Multiple Intelligences

GRADE **5**

teaching kids the way they learn

written by
Jennifer Overend Prior, M. Ed.

Cover by Dawn Devries Sokol
Interior illustrations by Mike Denman and Roberta Collier-Morales
Symbol design by Rose Sheifer

FS-23284 Multiple Intelligences: Teaching Kids the Way They Learn Grade 5
All rights reserved. Printed in the U.S.A.
Copyright © 1999 Frank Schaffer Publications, Inc.
23740 Hawthorne Blvd., Torrance, CA 90505

TABLE of CONTENTS

What Is the Multiple Intelligences Theory?

The Multiple Intelligences Theory, developed and researched by Dr. Howard Gardner, recognizes the multifaceted profile of the human mind. In his book *Frames of Mind* (Basic Books, 1993) Dr. Gardner explains that every human possesses several intelligences in greater or lesser degrees. Each person is born with a unique intelligence profile and uses any or all of these intelligences to acquire knowledge and experience.

At present Gardner has defined eight intelligences. Below are the intelligences and a simplified definition of each. A more complete explanation of each intelligence is found at the end of the introduction.

- verbal-linguistic: word intelligence
- logical-mathematical: number and reasoning intelligence
- visual-spatial: picture intelligence
- musical: music and rhythm intelligence
- bodily-kinesthetic: body intelligence
- interpersonal: social intelligence
- intrapersonal: self intelligence
- naturalist: natural environment intelligence

Gardner stresses that although intelligence is a biological function, it is inseparable from the cultural context in which it exists. He cites the example of Bobby Fischer, the chess champion. In a culture without chess, Fischer would not have been able to become a good chess player.

The Multiple Intelligences Theory in the Classroom

The Multiple Intelligences Theory has been making its way into the educational setting over the past decade. Instinctively, educators have recognized that their students learn differently, respond uniquely to a variety of teaching techniques, and have their individual preferences. Traditional educational programs do not recognize the unique intelligence profile of each student. Traditionally educators have operated according to the belief that there is a single type of intelligence, based on a combination of math and verbal ability. This more one-dimensional view gave rise to the commonly held definition of an "IQ." According to this definition, all individuals are born with this general ability and it does not change with age, training, or experience. Dr. Gardner's theory plays a significant role in rethinking how to educate so as to meet each student's individual needs. Basic skills can be more effectively acquired if all of a student's strengths are involved in the learning process.

The key to lesson design for a multiple intelligences learning environment is to reflect on the concept you want to teach and identify the intelligences that seem most appropriate for communicating the content. At Mountlake Terrace High School in Edmonds, Washington, Eeva Reeder's math students learn about algebraic equations kinesthetically by using the pavement in the school's yard like a giant graph. Using the large, square cement blocks of the pavement, they identify the axes, the X and Y coordinates, and plot themselves as points on the axes.

Other teachers will attempt to engage all eight intelligences in their lessons by using learning centers to focus on different approaches to the same concept. An example of this is Bruce Campbell's third grade classroom in Marysville, Washington. Campbell, a consultant on teaching through multiple intelligences, has designed a unit on Planet Earth that includes seven centers: a building center where students use clay to make models of the earth; a math center; a reading center; a music center where students study unit spelling words while listening to music; an art center using concentric circle patterns; a cooperative learning activity; a writing center titled "Things I would take with me on a journey to the center of the earth."

Another way to use the multiple intelligences theory in the classroom is through student projects. For example, Barbara Hoffman had her third-grade students in Country Day School in Costa Rica develop games in small groups. The students had to determine the objective and rules of the game. They researched questions and answers and designed and assembled a game board and accessories. Many intelligences were engaged through the creation of this project.

Dr. Gardner recommends that schools personalize their programs by providing apprenticeships. These should be designed to allow students to pursue their interests, with an emphasis on acquiring expertise over a period of time. In the Escuela Internacional Valle del Sol in Costa Rica, apprenticeships based on the eight intelligences are used. In one program long-term special subjects are offered to students in areas such as cooking, soccer, and drama. In addition, at the end of the term the entire school participates in a special project in multiage grouping with activities focused around a theme such as Egypt or European medieval life.

Assessment

The multiple intelligences theory challenges us to redefine assessment and see it as an integral part of the learning process. Dr. Gardner believes that many of the intelligences do not lend themselves to being measured by standardized paper and pencil tests. In a classroom structured on the multiple intelligences theory, assessment is integrated with learning and instruction and stimulates further learning. The teacher, the student, and his or her peers are involved in ongoing assessment. In this way the student has a better understanding of his or her strengths and weaknesses. Self-evaluation gives students the opportunity to set goals, to use higher-order thinking skills, as well as to generalize and personalize what they learn.

One example of nontraditional assessment is the development and maintenance of student portfolios, including drafts, sketches, and final products. Both student and teacher choose pieces that illustrate the student's growth. (Gardner calls these *process folios*.) Self-assessment can also include parental assessment, as well as watching videotaped student performances, and students editing or reviewing each other's work.

How to Use This Book

Multiple Intelligences: Teaching Kids the Way They Learn Grade 5 is designed to assist teachers in implementing this theory across the curriculum. This book is for teachers of students in fifth grade. It is divided into six subject areas: language arts, social studies, mathematics, science, fine arts, and physical education. Each subject area offers a collection of practical, creative ideas for teaching each of the eight intelligences. The book also offers reproducible student worksheets to supplement many of these activities. (A small image of the worksheet can be found next to the activity it supplements. Answers are provided at the end of the book.) Teachers may pick and choose from the various activities to develop a multiple intelligences program that meets their students' needs.

The activities are designed to help the teacher engage all the intelligences during the learning process so that the unique qualities of each student are recognized, encouraged, and cultivated. The activities provide opportunities for students to explore their individual interests and talents while learning the basic knowledge and skills that all must master. Each activity focuses on one intelligence; however, other intelligences will come into play since the intelligences naturally interact with each other.

As a teacher, you have the opportunity to provide a variety of educational experiences that can help students excel in their studies as well as discover new and exciting abilities and strengths within themselves. Your role in the learning process can provide students with an invaluable opportunity to fulfill their potential and enrich their lives.

Words of Advice

The following are some tips to assist you in using the Multiple Intelligences Theory in your classroom.

- Examine your own strengths and weaknesses in each of the intelligences. Call on others to help you expand your lessons to address the entire range of intelligences.

- Spend time in the early weeks of the school year working with your students to evaluate their comfort and proficiency within the various intelligences. Use your knowledge of their strengths to design and implement your teaching strategies.

- Refrain from "pigeonholing" your students into limited areas of intelligence. Realize that a student can grow from an activity that is not stressing his or her dominant intelligence.

- Work on goal-setting with students and help them develop plans to attain their goals.

- Develop a variety of assessment strategies and record-keeping tools.

- Flexibility is essential. The Multiple Intelligences Theory can be applied in a myriad of ways. There is no one right way.

The Eight Intelligences

Below is a brief definition of each of the eight intelligences, along with tips on how to recognize the characteristics of each and how to develop these intelligences in your students.

Verbal-Linguistic Intelligence

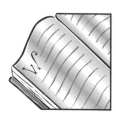

Verbal-linguistic intelligence consists of:

- a sensitivity to semantics—the meaning of words

- a sensitivity to syntax—the order among words

- a sensitivity to phonology—the sounds, rhythms, and inflections of words

- a sensitivity to the different functions of language, including its potential to excite, convince, stimulate, convey information, or please

Verbal-linguistic intelligence consists of the ability to think in words and to use words effectively, whether orally or in writing. The foundation of this intelligence is laid before birth, when the fetus develops hearing while still in the womb. It continues to develop after birth. Authors, poets, newscasters, journalists, public speakers, and playwrights are people who exhibit high degrees of linguistic intelligence.

People who are strongly linguistic like to read, write, tell stories or jokes, and play word games. They enjoy listening to stories or to people talking. They may have a good vocabulary or a good memory for names, places, dates, and trivia. They may spell words accurately and communicate to others effectively. They might also exhibit the ability to learn other languages.

Verbal-linguistic intelligence can be stimulated and developed in the classroom by providing a language rich environment. Classrooms in every subject area should include activities to help students develop a passion for language through speaking, hearing, reading, and examining words. Have students write stories, poems, jokes, letters, or journals. Provide opportunities for impromptu speaking, rapping, debate, storytelling, oral reading, silent reading, choral reading, and oral presentations. Involve students in class discussions and encourage them to ask questions and listen. Invite students to use storyboards, tape recorders, and word processors. Plan field trips to libraries, newspapers, or bookstores. Supply nontraditional materials such as comics and crossword puzzles to interest reluctant students.

Writing, listening, reading, and speaking effectively are key skills. The development of these four parts of linguistic intelligence can have a significant effect on a student's success in learning all subject areas and throughout life.

Logical-Mathematical Intelligence

Logical-mathematical intelligence consists of:

- the ability to use numbers effectively

- the ability to use inductive and deductive reasoning

- the ability to recognize abstract patterns

This intelligence encompasses three broad, interrelated fields: math, science, and logic. It begins when young children confront the physical objects of the world and ends with the understanding of abstract ideas. Throughout this process, a person develops a capacity to discern logical or numerical patterns and to handle long chains of reasoning. Scientists, mathematicians, computer programmers, bankers, accountants, and lawyers exhibit high degrees of logical-mathematical intelligence.

People with well-developed logical-mathematical intelligence like to find patterns and relationships among objects or numbers. They enjoy playing strategy games such as chess or checkers and solving riddles, logical puzzles, or brain teasers. They organize or categorize things and ask questions about how things work. These people easily solve math problems quickly in their heads. They may have a good sense of cause and effect and think on a more abstract or conceptual level.

Logical-mathematical intelligence can be stimulated and developed in the classroom by providing an environment in which students frequently experiment, classify, categorize, and analyze. Have students notice and work with numbers across the curriculum. Provide activities that focus on outlining, analogies, deciphering codes, or finding patterns and relationships.

Most adults use logical-mathematical intelligence in their daily lives to calculate household budgets, to make decisions, and to solve problems. Most professions depend in some way on this intelligence because it encompasses many kinds of thinking. The development of logical-mathematical intelligence benefits all aspects of life.

Bodily-Kinesthetic Intelligence

Bodily-kinesthetic intelligence consists of:

- the ability to control one's body movements to express ideas and feelings
- the capacity to handle objects skillfully, including the use of both fine and gross motor movements
- the ability to learn by movement, interaction, and participation

Bodily-kinesthetic intelligence begins with the control of automatic and voluntary movement and progresses to using the body in highly differentiated ways. The skillful manipulation of one's body or an object requires an acute sense of timing and direction, as well as the ability to transform an intention into action. Examples of people who possess bodily-kinesthetic intelligence are a dancer using his or her body as an object for expressive purposes and a basketball player who manipulates a ball with finesse. This intelligence can be seen in inventors, mechanics, actors, surgeons, swimmers, and artists.

People who are strongly bodily-kinesthetic enjoy working with their hands, have good coordination, and handle tools skillfully. They enjoy taking things apart and putting them back together. They prefer to manipulate objects to solve problems. They move, twitch, tap, or fidget while seated for a long time. They cleverly mimic other's gestures.

Many people find it difficult to understand and retain information that is taught only through their visual and auditory modes. They must manipulate or experience what they learn in order to understand and remember information. Bodily-kinesthetic individuals learn through doing and through multi-sensory experiences.

Bodily-kinesthetic intelligence can be stimulated and developed in the classroom through activities that involve physical movements such as role-playing, drama, mime, charades, dance, sports, and exercise. Have your students put on plays, puppet shows, or dance performances. Provide opportunities for students to manipulate and touch objects through activities such as painting, clay modeling, or building. Plan field trips to the theater, art museum, ballet, craft shows, and parks.

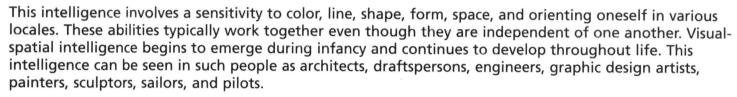

Visual-Spatial Intelligence

Visual-spatial intelligence consists of:

- the ability to perceive the visual-spatial world accurately
- the ability to think in pictures or visual imagery
- the ability to graphically represent visual or spatial ideas
- the ability to orient the body in space

This intelligence involves a sensitivity to color, line, shape, form, space, and orienting oneself in various locales. These abilities typically work together even though they are independent of one another. Visual-spatial intelligence begins to emerge during infancy and continues to develop throughout life. This intelligence can be seen in such people as architects, draftspersons, engineers, graphic design artists, painters, sculptors, sailors, and pilots.

Spatially skilled people enjoy art activities, jigsaw or visual perception puzzles, and mazes. They like to construct three-dimensional models. These people get more out of pictures than words in reading materials. They may excel at reading maps, charts, and diagrams. Also, they may have a good sense of direction.

Visual-spatial intelligence can be stimulated and developed in the classroom by providing a visually rich environment in which students frequently focus on images, pictures, and color. Provide opportunities for reading maps and charts, drawing diagrams and illustrations, constructing models, painting, coloring, and solving puzzles. Play games that require visual memory or spatial acuity. Use guided imagery, pretending, or active imagination exercises to have students solve problems. Use videos, slides, posters, charts, diagrams, telescopes, or color-coded material to teach the content area. Visit art museums, historical buildings, or planetariums.

Visual-spatial intelligence is an object-based intelligence. It functions in the concrete world, the world of objects and their locations. This intelligence underlies all human activity.

Musical Intelligence

Musical intelligence consists of:

- a sensitivity to pitch (melody), rhythm, and timbre (tone)
- an appreciation of musical expressiveness
- an ability to express oneself through music, rhythm, or dance

Dr. Gardner asserts that of all forms of intelligence, the consciousness-altering effect of musical intelligence is probably the greatest because of the impact of music on the state of the brain. He suggests that many individuals who have had frequent exposure to music can manipulate pitch, rhythm, and timbre to participate with some skill in composing, singing, or playing instruments. The early childhood years appear to be the most crucial period for musical growth. This intelligence can be seen in composers, conductors, instrumentalists, singers, and dancers.

Musically skilled people may remember the melodies of songs. They may have a good singing voice and tap rhythmically on a surface. Also, they may unconsciously hum to themselves and may be able to identify when musical notes are off-key. They enjoy singing songs, listening to music, playing an instrument, or attending musical performances.

Musical intelligence can be stimulated and developed in the classroom by providing opportunities to listen to musical recordings, to create and play musical instruments, or to sing and dance. Let students express their feelings or thoughts through using musical instruments, songs, or jingles. Play background music while the students are working. Plan field trips to the symphony, a recording studio, a musical, or an opera.

There are strong connections between music and emotions. By having music in the classroom, a positive emotional environment conducive to learning can be created. Lay the foundations of musical intelligence in your classroom by using music throughout the school day.

Interpersonal Intelligence

Interpersonal intelligence consists of:

- the ability to focus outward to other individuals
- the ability to sense other people's moods, temperaments, motivations, and intentions
- the ability to communicate, cooperate, and collaborate with others

In the early form of this intelligence, a young child possesses the ability to discriminate among the individuals around him or her and to detect their various moods. In the more advanced form of this intelligence, one can read the intentions and desires of other individuals and act upon that knowledge. This intelligence includes the ability to form and maintain relationships and to assume various roles within groups. The competence is prominent in political and religious leaders, salespeople, teachers, counselors, social workers, and therapists.

Interpersonally skilled people have the capacity to influence their peers and often excel at group work, team efforts, and collaborative projects. They enjoy social interaction and are sensitive to the feelings and moods of others. They tend to take leadership roles in activities with friends and often belong to clubs and other organizations.

Interpersonal intelligence can be developed and strengthened through maintaining a warm, accepting, supporting classroom environment. Provide opportunities for students to collaboratively work in groups. Have students peer teach and contribute to group discussions. Involve the students in situations where they have to be active listeners, be aware of other's feelings, motives, and opinions, and show empathy.

The positive development of interpersonal intelligence is an important step toward leading a successful and fulfilling life. Interpersonal intelligence is called upon in our daily lives as we interact with others in our communities, environments, nations, and world.

Intrapersonal Intelligence

Intrapersonal intelligence consists of:

- the ability to look inward to examine one's own thoughts and feelings
- the ability to control one's thoughts and emotions and consciously work with them
- the ability to express one's inner life
- the drive toward self-actualization

This intelligence focuses on the ability to develop a complete model of oneself, including one's desires, goals, anxieties, strengths, and limitations, and also to draw upon that model as a means of understanding and guiding one's behavior. In its basic form, it is the ability to distinguish a feeling of pleasure from one of pain, and to make a determination to either continue or withdraw from a situation based on this feeling. In the more advanced form of this intelligence, one has the ability to detect and to symbolize complex and highly differentiated sets of feelings. Some individuals with strong intrapersonal intelligence are philosophers, spiritual counselors, psychiatrists, and wise elders.

Intrapersonally skilled people are aware of their range of emotions and have a realistic sense of their strengths and weaknesses. They prefer to work independently and often have their own style of living and learning. They are able to accurately express their feelings and have a good sense of self-direction. They possess high self-confidence.

Intrapersonal intelligence can be developed through maintaining a warm, caring, nurturing environment that promotes self-esteem. Offer activities that require independent learning and imagination. During the school day, provide students with quiet time and private places to work and reflect. Provide long-term, meaningful learning projects that allow students to explore their interests and abilities. Encourage students to maintain portfolios and examine and make sense of their work. Involve students in activities that require them to explore their values, beliefs, and feelings.

Intrapersonal intelligence requires a lifetime of living and learning to inwardly know, be, and accept oneself. The classroom is a place where teachers can help students begin this journey of self-knowledge. Developing intrapersonal intelligence has far-reaching effects, since self-knowledge underlies success and fulfillment in life.

Naturalist Intelligence

Naturalist intelligence consists of:

- the ability to understand, appreciate, and enjoy the natural world
- the ability to observe, understand, and organize patterns in the natural environment
- the ability to nurture plants and animals

This intelligence focuses on the ability to recognize and classify the many different organic and inorganic species. Paleontologists, forest rangers, horticulturists, zoologists, and meteorologists exhibit naturalist intelligence.

People who exhibit strength in the naturalist intelligence are very much at home in nature. They enjoy being outdoors, camping, and hiking, as well as studying and learning about animals and plants. They can easily classify and identify various species.

Naturalist intelligence can be developed and strengthened through activities that involve hands-on labs, creating classroom habitats, caring for plants and animals, and classifying and discriminating species. Encourage your students to collect and classify seashells, insects, rocks, or other natural phenomena. Visit a museum of natural history, a university life sciences department, or nature center.

Naturalist intelligence enhances our lives. The more we know about the natural world, and the more we are able to recognize patterns in our environment, the better perspective we have on our role in natural cycles and our place in the universe.

REFERENCES

Armstrong, Thomas. *Multiple Intelligences in the Classroom*. Alexandria, VA: Assoc. for Supervision and Curriculum Development, 1994. A good overview of the Multiple Intelligences Theory and how to explore, introduce, and develop lessons on this theory.

Campbell, Linda, Bruce Campbell, and Dee Dickerson. *Teaching and Learning Through Multiple Intelligences*. Needham Heights, MA: Allyn and Bacon, 1996. An overview and resource of teaching strategies in musical, spatial, bodily-kinesthetic, interpersonal, and intrapersonal intelligences.

Gardner, Howard. *Frames of Mind: The Theory of Multiple Intelligences*. New York: Basic Books, 1993. A detailed analysis and explanation of the Multiple Intelligences Theory.

———. *Multiple Intelligences: The Theory in Practice*. New York: Basic Books, 1993. This book provides a coherent picture of what Gardner and his colleagues have learned about the educational applications of the Multiple Intelligences Theory over the last decade. It provides an overview of the theory and examines its implications for assessment and teaching from preschool to college admissions.

Haggerty, Brian A. *Nurturing Intelligences: A Guide to Multiple Intelligences Theory and Teaching*. Menlo Park, CA: Innovative Learning, Addison-Wesley, 1995. Principles, practical suggestions, and examples for applying the Multiple Intelligences Theory in the classroom. Exercises, problems, and puzzles introduce each of the seven intelligences.

Lazear, David. *Seven Pathways of Learning: Teaching Students and Parents About Multiple Intelligences*. Tucson: Zephyr Press, 1994. Assists in strengthening the child's personal intelligence and in integrating multiple intelligences into everyday life. Includes reproducibles and activities to involve parents.

———. *Seven Ways of Knowing: Teaching for Multiple Intelligences*. Arlington Heights, IL: IRI/SkyLight Training, 1992. A survey of the theory of multiple intelligences with many general activities for awakening and developing the intelligences.

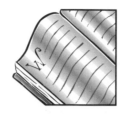

Verbal-Linguistic
Intelligence

Silly Sentences

This is a fun way for students to practice creating proper sentences using different parts of speech. Label each of five envelopes with a different part of speech—*nouns, verbs, adjectives, pronouns,* and *articles.* In each envelope place several strips of paper labeled with various words for that category. To create silly sentences, students work individually or in pairs, removing word strips from the envelopes and sequencing them to create sentences. Completed sentences should be copied onto a sheet of paper to share with other students.

Instant Poets

This thought-provoking activity allows students to write about their views of life in an abstract way. Discuss with your students the difference between metaphors and similes. Give examples of similes, such as *Her hair is like gold thread, His eyes were like blue marbles.* An example of a metaphor would be "The day was a circus." This is a good time to explain what a mixed metaphor is, and to avoid sentences such as *Don't let the moss grow under your feet while you're crossing that bridge.*

Explain to your students that metaphors and similes can, when successful, describe something much more succinctly than a long discourse. Poets use metaphor and simile, and in this activity your students can become instant poets. Ask students to think of metaphors to describe their feelings about events, people, memories, etc. Have each student make a list of ten of these kinds of topics and create metaphors and similes to describe them.

Literary Newsletter

To accompany your next book unit, have each student create a literary newsletter reporting events from the chapter book read in class. As students read the book, have them take notes about interesting events, facts, and details that might be developed into newsletter articles.

Print a newsletter template for each student from a computer program such as ClarisWorks (Claris Corporation) or Microsoft Word (Microsoft). The student can then write articles for each section. Articles for the newsletter could include news stories, feature stories, and editorials. Outline various types of stories to use as guidelines for writing. A news story tells who, what, when, where, how, and why. It also includes important facts and details. A feature story appeals to human interest and is written in an exciting, narrative format. An editorial deals with opinions about an issue or an event. It presents relevant facts and details as well as the writer's opinions.

Operation: Definition

Put creativity to work with this fun dictionary game. Students play the game in groups of four or five. To begin, one student takes the role of the leader and chooses an uncommon word from the dictionary and reads it to the group. The leader writes the real definition on a piece of paper. The other students each make up a definition for the word and write it on a piece of paper. The true and fictional definitions are all placed randomly in a pile and then each one is read aloud by the leader. Students take turns guessing which one is the actual dictionary definition of the word. A point is awarded to each student who chooses the correct definition. Additional points are awarded to students whose fictional definitions were chosen by other children in the group. Play continues in this manner with a different child taking the role of the leader during each round.

Word Predictions

As students read a chapter book in class, have them record unfamiliar words and the page numbers where they were found using the reproducible on page 20, **Word Prediction Chart.** Have students write what they think each word means by using context clues. Then have each student share his or her unfamiliar words in small groups. Have each student read a sentence containing one of the words and then have groups discuss their thoughts on the word's meaning. After listening to all of the ideas, students should use the dictionary to find the actual meaning of the word and record it on the chart.

Character Poem

Have each student choose a favorite character from a book to be the subject of a poem. Using the format below, the student completes each line from the point-of-view of the character. To create the poem, the words should be written on a piece of paper, without the prompt lines below.

Line 1: Character's Name

Line 2: I live...

Line 3: I can...

Line 4: I enjoy...

Line 5: I feel...

Line 6: I am unique because...

page 20

Logical-Mathematical Intelligence

Story Game Boards

In this activity, students demonstrate their knowledge of story events while constructing unique game boards. The game boards should be based on books the class is familiar with. Have students work in groups to draw a game board path on a large piece of construction paper or tagboard. Allow students to determine how players will progress along the game path using a spinner or dice. Each space on the game path could contain a story event with an instruction to move forward or backward. For example, "Maniac Magee scores 49 touchdowns. Move ahead two spaces." Spaces could also refer players to question cards pertaining to story events. The accuracy of the answer determines the player's ability to lose a turn or take another turn. Student groups can take turns playing other groups' games.

Story Sleuths

While engaged in a unit based on a novel, encourage students to make predictions about future events in the story. As a group, have students brainstorm their predictions as you list each one on chart paper. Ask students to name facts in the story that lead them to make these predictions. List the facts below each prediction on the chart. As students read the book, have them compare the story events to their predictions. Allow students to change or fine-tune predictions.

Ad Assessment

How do advertisements entice people to purchase products? Have your students evaluate a variety of ads to find out. Provide several copies of newspapers and magazines. Have students tear out different types of manufacturers' ads. Ask students to identify the words, phrases, and graphics that create visual appeal. They should then decide what type of audience the advertisement is attempting to reach. Is the ad appealing to adults, teenagers, or students? Is it directed toward men or women? Encourage students to explain the reasons for their answers.

Bodily-Kinesthetic
Intelligence

What Really Matters?

When focusing on a particular book character, ask students to think about the things that are important to that character. Have students brainstorm the people, places, and objects that the character values and list these responses on chart paper. Then have each student form several of these objects using salt dough. (See the recipe below.) Place salt-dough formations on wax paper in a well-ventilated area to dry. After several days of drying, the salt dough can be painted with watercolor or tempera paint. Have students label and display their creations for classmates to see.

Salt Dough Recipe:

1 cup salt

2 cups flour

1 cup water

Mix ingredients in a bowl and knead until smooth. If the dough is too soft, add a bit more flour. If it is too stiff, add small amounts of water.

Make the Scene

Choose a book for students to read that has a great deal of dialogue in it. As students read the book, ask them to consider which of the scenes in the book they would like to act out with one or more other students. They should make note of this scene. Then, after all students have finished reading the book, have them give their ideas for scenes to act out. List these on chart paper. Undoubtedly, some students will choose the same scene. Now, assign students into groups to perform some of the favorite scenes. Students need not write out scripts. They should simply act it out as they remember what the characters said and did.

Visual-Spatial
Intelligence

Story Photo Album

Here's an eye-catching way to display story events or settings. Have each student list several important events or settings in a story. Invite each student to discuss his or her list with classmates to recall details about the scenery or actions that took place. Then, on each of several unlined index cards, have the students draw one of the listed items using colored pencils. Prompt the student to draw detailed pictures to appear like photographs. When the "photos" are complete, students can attach them sequentially to heavy-stock pages in a binder and label each photo in reference to the story.

Setting Maps

Understanding a story's setting is essential to comprehension. As students read or listen to a story, ask them to make notes about where the events take place. Once the story setting is well established, have each student create a map of event locations. Prompt the student to include important streets, buildings, bodies of water, or land masses. When the map is complete, have the students label areas of the map with events that occurred in those locations. Allow students the opportunity to compare their maps and discuss their individual perceptions.

Multi-Picture Author Frame

Here's a fun and artistic way to display knowledge of a book's author. Gather information about a selected author and, as a class, list interesting facts about him or her on chart paper. To begin, each student needs one white and one colored sheet of 9-by-14-inch construction paper. To create the multi-picture frame, the student cuts out five or six large shapes from the colored sheet of construction paper. Cutout shapes are discarded and the colored sheet is glued on top of a white sheet, the edges aligned. In each of the framed areas, the student draws a picture to represent a piece of information about the author. Each picture should be labeled with the fact.

Musical Intelligence

A Chorus of Voices

Introduce the word *chorus* and ask a volunteer to define it. Help students realize that a presentation by a chorus doesn't necessarily have to be sung. The word describes something done in unison by a group, such as a chorus line of dancers, or a group speaking in one voice. Ask students to consider what choral presentations have in common, helping them to see that understanding rhythm and tempo are important to any kind of activity done in unison.

Invite students to do a choral reading in two parts. Explain that it is important to practice so the words sound musical—spoken in unison with a pleasing rhythm and tempo. Begin by dividing a poem such as "The Little Turtle" by Vachel Lindsay into speaking parts by alternating every line. Or choose a reading from *Joyful Noise: Poems for Two Voices,* by Paul Fleishman (HarperCollins, 1988).

Parts-of-Speech Jingle

Learning about the English language is fun when set to a catchy tune. Ask students to think about rules for using parts of speech or punctuation. Then have them write a few stanzas about how to use them properly. Stanzas may or may not rhyme. Students complete their projects by creating a tune with which to sing their jingles. Allow students to teach their jingles to classmates to help with future language activities.

Tongue Twister Tunes

Read to the class *Six Sick Sheep: 101 Tongue Twisters,* by Joanna Cole and Stephanie Calmenson (Scholastic, 1993). Encourage students to try to say several of the tongue twisters in the book. Then ask students to choose one tongue twister to set to music. Ask students if they find the tongue twister easier or harder to say when sung to a tune. Invite students to teach their fun songs to other students in your school.

 **Interpersonal Intelligence**

Vocabulary Crossword

Motivate students to increase their vocabulary with crossword fun. Pair off students and present a different set of vocabulary words to each pair. Students will work in pairs to create their crossword puzzles. First have students use the dictionary to determine word definitions. Then have students create a list of clues. Next students create the actual puzzle, numbering the boxes across and down. When all students have created their puzzles, have them trade puzzles with other students. Students again work in pairs, using the dictionary when needed, to complete the crossword puzzles.

Group Silly Stories

Students create amusing stories with this shared writing experience. Divide your class into groups of four or five. To begin, each child thinks of an original story character and writes the first portion of a story with that character. When all students are finished, they pass the stories to a different group member. Then students add to their classmates' stories. Students continue in this manner until each group member has written a part of each story. Remind students to write conclusions when they receive the last stories. After the stories are complete, invite students to share their completed creations by reading them aloud to the entire class.

Decisions, Decisions

Throughout the reading of a selected book, list the decisions that the main character makes. Choose one of the decisions and, as a class, discuss different choices that could have been made by the character. Discuss the series of events that took place based on that decision. Encourage students to think about how a different decision would have effected the outcome of the story. Then have students gather in small groups, change one of the character's decisions, and create an alternate turn of events for the story based on this change.

 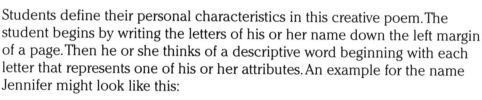

Intrapersonal Intelligence

A Novel Friendship

When reading a book containing several characters, have students keep a list of their impressions of each one. When they have finished reading the book, have students choose one of the characters to be their friend. Have students write an essay about what they'd do with their new friend. Would they write to the character, take him or her on a tour of their home, bring him or her to school? The essay should describe the students themselves like a character, and can include dialogue.

Introspective Acrostics

Students define their personal characteristics in this creative poem. The student begins by writing the letters of his or her name down the left margin of a page. Then he or she thinks of a descriptive word beginning with each letter that represents one of his or her attributes. An example for the name Jennifer might look like this:

Jolly

Energetic

Nice

Noisy

Imaginative

Fun-loving

Exuberant

Radiant

If I Were in Charge of the World

Read the poem "If I Were in Charge of the World" from the book *If I Were in Charge of the World and Other Worries,* by Judith Viorst (Aladdin Books, 1981). Then have students think about what they would do if they could be in charge of the world. Duplicate and distribute copies of the student worksheet **If I Were in Charge of the World**, on page 21. Ask students to complete the page to create poems of their own.

page 21

Personal Journal Topics

Journal writing is a great way to express personal feelings each day. Keep your students motivated to write with a variety of topics such as:

- My most valued possession...
- I'm worried about...
- You would never believe this about me...
- My hero is...
- I am most afraid of...
- What I think about the future...
- I'm really good at...
- What my friends like most about me is...

How's My Writing?

Encourage students to periodically evaluate their own writing in order to assess their progress. After students review their writing, ask them to make any necessary changes. Give students the questions below to consider for their self-evaluations. You may want to arrange these questions in the form of a checklist.

- Did I write clearly?
- Did I provide enough information?
- Did I have a clear beginning and ending?
- Are my ideas in a logical order?
- Will my readers understand what I wrote?
- Did I use any creative words or phrases?
- Is my story easy to read?
- Did I use proper punctuation and capitalization?
- Did I spell all of the words correctly?

page 22

If I Were a...

With this project, students compare their personal qualities to common objects, feelings, and colors. To create a unique, introspective poem, have each child complete the phrases on the student worksheet **If I Were a . . .** on page 22. Encourage students to include additional lines to the poem, as desired. The words written on the lines can be copied onto another piece of paper to create the poem. Students can put the poem on colored construction paper and create a border.

Are You Dreamy?

Dreams can be happy, sad, strange, scary. Whatever type they are, most people think dreams are quite interesting. Ask students to recall a dream they have had recently. Have each student record the details of the dream on a sheet of paper. Encourage them to write down any questions they have about the dream or gaps in the sequence of events. Then have each child write the dream in the form of a story, augmented with imaginary events to add to the story's plot.

Naturalist Intelligence

Biodiversity

Study biodiversity with your class by reading *Living Treasure: Saving Earth's Threatened Biodiversity,* by Laurence Pringle (Morrow, 1991). Other good resources are *Biodiversity,* by Dorothy Henshaw Patent (Clarion, 1996), and *Bats, Bugs, and Biodiversity: Adventures in the Amazonian Rain Forest,* by Susan Goodman (Atheneum, 1995).

Explain to your class that humans also exhibit the characteristics of biodiversity; some have freckles, some have red hair, some are green eyed, etc.

Create a biodiversity display in your classroom that can be developed throughout the year. Start by observing the human biodiversity in the classroom. Take photos of some students' hands, some students' eyes, others' smiles. Make sure all children are represented. Mount these photos for all to appreciate each person's individuality.

Add to the biodiversity display by having students collect any of the following: seashells, pine cones, leaves, bugs, nuts, feathers, and other objects from nature. Point out to students that there is diversity within each species as well as among them.

Sharp Senses

To give your students an opportunity to "stop and smell the roses" and put the experience into words, offer them copies of the **Sharp Senses** worksheet found on page 23. As a homework assignment, have them choose a spot outdoors for observation and record what they see, hear, touch, smell, and taste. (Point out that many observation opportunities will not involve taste, and that section may be blank.) Have students keep their completed forms and ask them to refer to them during the class's next creative writing exercise.

Nature Word Flowers

A simple flower drawing can serve as a tool for expanding your students' vocabulary while increasing their awareness of nature. Choose a topic related to the natural world and write it in a flower shape. Then add stem and leaf lines to the flower for words related to that topic. The example at right is based on the theme "Nature Sounds." Students added the words *whoosh, screech, plunk, rumble, giggle* to describe the sound the nouns on the left make. Keep the completed flower, and other word flowers created by the class, on display so they can be referred to during reading and writing time.

page 23

Name _____

Word Prediction Chart

As you read a book, record unfamiliar words on this chart. Also include the page number on which the word was found. Look at the word in context. What do you think it means? Write your prediction under "Predicted Definition." Then look up the word and write down the dictionary definition. Did you make a good guess?

Title of Book: _____

Word: _____   Page number: _____

Predicted Definition:

_____

_____

_____

Dictionary Definition:

_____

_____

_____

Word: _____   Page number: _____

Predicted Definition:

_____

_____

_____

Dictionary Definition:

_____

_____

_____

Word: _____   Page number: _____

Predicted Definition:

_____

_____

_____

Dictionary Definition:

_____

_____

_____

LANGUAGE ARTS
Verbal-Linguistic Intelligence

If I Were in Charge of the World

Wouldn't it be great to be in charge of the world? Complete the statements below describing what you would do if you were in charge of the world.

If I were in charge of the world, I'd cancel

_____, _____,

and _____.

If I were in charge of the world, there'd be

_____, _____,

and _____.

If I were in charge of the world, everyone could

_____, _____,

and _____.

If I were in charge of the world, these things would be free:

_____, _____,

and _____.

If I were in charge of the world

_____

_____

_____

_____

_____

_____

_____

_____

_____

_____

_____

_____.

LANGUAGE ARTS
Intrapersonal Intelligence

If I Were a...

Let your imagination go wild! Complete the phrases below to create a unique, introspective poem.

If I were a color, I'd be

_____.

If I were a song, I'd be

_____.

If I were a food, I'd be

_____.

If I were a car, I'd be

_____.

If I were an animal, I'd be

_____.

If I were a place, I'd be

_____.

If I were a feeling, I'd be

_____.

If a were a plant, I'd be

_____.

If I were a climate, I'd be

_____.

If I were a musical instrument, I'd be

_____.

If I were a shape, I'd be

_____.

LANGUAGE ARTS
Intrapersonal Intelligence

Sharp Senses

Successful writers are good observers who are always alert for new experiences. They use their senses as they react personally to these experiences. How does the snow sound underfoot? What does fresh-baked bread smell like? How does the surface of a warm woolen coat feel? These are all observations a writer might make and use later when describing something in a story.

Improve your observation powers by sharpening your senses. Go for a walk or find a quiet place to sit and observe. Then record everything your senses tell you about the experience. Write your observations in colorful detail so you will remember them. Don't just record that you heard the sound of water. Instead, describe the sound. Was the water rushing, trickling, or dripping? Later, use some of the observations in your own writing.

My observation experience:

_____

Sights: _____

_____

_____

Sounds: _____

_____

_____

Textures: _____

_____

_____

Smells: _____

_____

_____

Tastes: _____

_____

_____

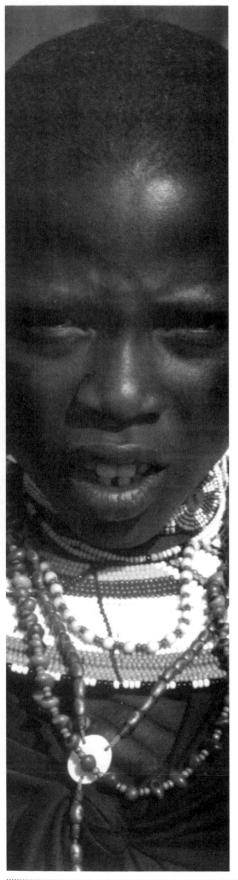

Verbal-Linguistic Intelligence

The Gettysburg Address

During the Civil War, more American lives were taken than in any other war in history. This war, which was fought in its entirety on American soil, was an important turning point in the history of our country. After learning about the Civil War, provide students with copies of The Gettysburg Address, delivered by President Abraham Lincoln on November 19, 1863. (Access the following web site for a copy of the address:

http://jefferson.village.virginia.edu/readings/gettysburg.txt)

In small groups, have students read the address and discuss the meaning of Lincoln's words in reference to the events of that time. Then have students write a few paragraphs explaining their interpretations of the message and the consequences for America's future.

Children in the Third World

As students study about third world countries, have them discuss the things that children in these countries do without every day. Ask them to brainstorm categories of basic need—such as food, water, shelter, and clothing—as you record their responses on a large sheet of chart paper. In each category, have students dictate the needs of children in the disadvantaged countries and the detrimental effects of being deprived of these necessities. Have students discuss the differences between wants and needs and how we view them in our country and in our personal lives. Ask each student to think about what they own and categorize it as either a want or a need.

News Around the World

Help your students stay aware of world news with this news-writing activity. To begin, provide students with several different newspapers to explore. Have each student find an article regarding news in another country. After they've read their articles, provide each student with a copy of the news article writing frame on page 32, **In the News.** On this page, the student writes the title of the original article and important details of the story. Then the student rewrites the article in his or her own words at the bottom of the page. Have pairs of students read and compare each other's articles and comment on the rewritten versions.

page 32

The Great Debate

Participating in a debate is a great way for students to learn about different sides of important issues. Decide on an issue for students to debate. For example:

- Should people be allowed to own hand guns?

- Should a factory that employs hundreds of people but pollutes the environment be allowed to stay in business?

- Should companies be allowed to test potentially harmful products on animals?

- Should there be a mandated curfew for children under the age of 18?

After deciding on a debate issue, divide your students into two teams based on their opinions. Have students in each group discuss the important points pertaining to their side and list them on personal copies of **The Great Debate** worksheet on page 33. Then have the team list the possible arguments that could be presented by the opposing team. Encourage students to brainstorm and list counterpoints for their opponents' arguments. After giving each team plenty of time to prepare, let the debate begin!

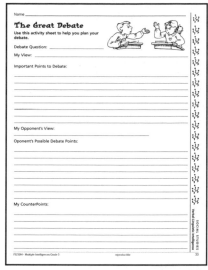

page 33

Logical-Mathematical Intelligence

Terrific Time Lines

Invite students to create a large time line based on some aspect of the social studies curriculum. For example, you may want them to create a time line of inventions, exploration, settlement of the United States, the Civil Rights movement, or another pertinent topic. Once the topic is determined, work with students to complete the time line as follows:

1. Identify the starting and ending dates for the time line.

2. Determine how to best subdivide the time line—into 1, 10, 20, 100 year periods, for example.

3. Measure the space available—a classroom or hallway wall, sheet of mural paper, large bulletin board, top of the chalkboard, etc.

4. Compute the amount of space that can be allotted to each time period and label the time line.

5. Assign small groups or individuals to specific time spans. Have them research appropriate facts to be included on the time line. Each item to be included should be labeled and illustrated on the time line itself, or on an index card that can be attached to the time line.

Bodily-Kinesthetic Intelligence

Foreign Foods

When learning about different countries, students are often interested in the types of foods eaten by other people. Divide students into small groups and have each group choose a type of food from a selected country. Have students take note of how foods reflect natural resources and geography. For example, an island cuisine would naturally include seafood. Countries that rely heavily on dairy products would have a large amount of pastureland. After finding a desired recipe, have each group determine the ingredients needed and how they will obtain them. Allow students to prepare the recipe at home or in a school kitchen and share the treats with classmates on an International Food Day. Encourage students to explain how the cuisine reflects the resources and geography of the country.

Homemade Toys

Discuss with students the many kinds of dolls on the market today. Explain that in the late 1800s, dolls were very simple, made of rags or even cornhusks. In Laura Ingalls Wilder's book *Little House in the Big Woods*, young Laura had a doll made out of a corncob. Have your children make their own dolls out of cornhusks.

Materials: To make a doll, each student needs eight dried cornhusks, three rubber bands, and markers or paint (optional).

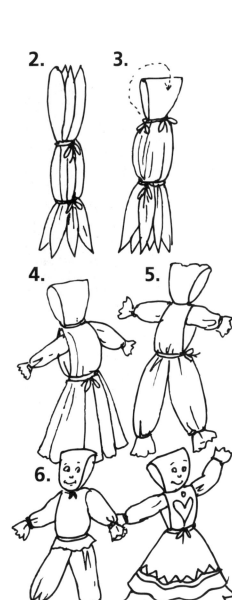

1. Soak the cornhusks in warm water for about an hour, until they are soft. Drain on paper towels.

2. Tie six husks together with string or rubberband around the middle to create a neck. Tie again about two inches below this to form the torso.

3. To create a face, fold the top of the husks down and tie at the same place that the top string was tied.

4. Create arms with hands by tying two husks together near the ends. Put the arms through the opening in the husks that forms the torso.

5. To make pants, cut the husks vertically below the waist. Tie each leg near the bottom.

6. Add facial features and decorative clothing with markers or paint, if desired.

Build a Native-American Home

After studying about different Native-American tribes, have students demonstrate knowledge of certain tribal homes with this construction activity. Have each student decide the kind of Native-American house he or she would like to make. Ask the student to determine the kinds of materials used to construct this type of house. Then have the student plan how the miniature house will be constructed. For example, if constructing a hogan, the student may decide to use sticks and a mixture of mud and dried grass, assembled on a board. Have students construct homes. Be sure to have them share their houses with classmates and describe how they were made.

Visual-Spatial Intelligence

Create a Continent

Here is a great way to apply knowledge of map skills. Tell children that they will each create their own fictional continent. This continent should have a variety of land forms, bodies of water, a name, cities, a capitol city, and major highways. Students may draw maps of their continents on poster board or create three-dimensional versions using salt dough. (A recipe can be found on page 13.) Remind students to create a map key and a legend to explain icons and objects on the map. Challenge students to create lines of longitude and latitude to show the continent's location. Then, based on the location, have students determine what the weather would be like on the continent and how this would influence the lives of the people who live there.

Map Skills

Improve map skills with this grid coordinate activity. To begin, give each student a sheet of grid paper. Then have each student draw a small house on each of three intersections. The student then determines which two houses are closest to each other and which two are farthest apart.

To extend this activity, have each student create a series of directions, from the starting point of $(0,0)$, and create a roundabout way of getting to one of the houses. For example, if the selected house is located at $(3,6)$, the directions might be:

- Go east 5 and north one.

- From that point, go north 3 and west 4.

- Now, go east 5 and south 1.

- You're home!

After writing the directions, have each student sit with a partner. Each student should have his or her list of directions, the grid marked with houses, and another blank grid. Each student takes a turn reading his or her directions, while the partner follows them and marks the location on the blank grid. He or she then compares the location of this house to the actual location on the partner's grid. If students do not find their way to the correct location, have them review the directions to determine any errors in their understanding. Then allow partners to reverse roles and continue in the same manner.

Musical Intelligence

Class Elections

When holding class elections during a unit about voting, enlist the musical assistance of some of your students. Have two or three students work together to create a campaign song for a chosen candidate in your classroom. Be sure to have the students interview the candidate so they can accurately portray the candidate's beliefs and plans once elected to office. After creating the song, have students make and distribute copies to classmates. Students can sing the songs together in support of their favorite candidates.

Country Music

What types of music do people in other countries listen to? This is a great way for students to find out. First students should choose a country. Then have each student locate music from this country. Your school library, music teacher, or public library may have useful resources. Students may also be able to locate videos about their countries that contain background music or dance performances. Allow students to listen to several songs from the selected country and choose a favorite. They can each share their discoveries with the class. As an example, have groups of students create dances to accompany the song. Encourage students to share and teach their dances to classmates. Allow students to perform their dances for other classes, parents, or administrators.

To extend the activity, have students analyze the components of a country's music and dance tradition and compare it to the music and dance of their own culture. Are there any tribal behaviors evident in today's pop culture? What role does music play in the students' society? Are there any similarities between the dances of their culture and that of the country they're studying? Compare and contrast the two culture's behavior.

Interpersonal Intelligence

Body Language

People communicate in many different ways. We often think of communication as spoken language, but what about body language?

Students can benefit from learning to read the body language of others. Ask students to observe conversations on the playground and other locations, such as the cafeteria or the library. As they observe, tell them to unobtrusively take notes regarding the students' body language. Do the observed students appear relaxed? Are their arms crossed in front of them? Are they leaning toward or away from their partners? Are they giving eye contact or glancing away frequently? As a class, discuss their observations and what various gestures and body positions may indicate. Invite students to watch the body language of students in other locations such as the cafeteria or the library. Have them observe the students they see and determine the messages being communicated through body language. Assemble students as a group to share their observations once again.

Situational Problem Solving

Handling conflict is often a difficult task. This activity helps children discuss various conflict situations and brainstorm solutions. Divide students into groups of four or five. Give each group a slip of paper with a conflict situation. Here are some suggestions:

- You are working on a group project. One of the group members refuses to participate and disrupts the work of the group. What do you do?

- You are working on an assignment in class and two students near you continue to whisper back and forth. You are having difficulty concentrating. What do you do?

- A student tells you that one of your friends has been saying mean things about you behind your back. How do you handle this?

Explain to students that when conflicts occur, it is a good idea to try and see the issue through the other person's eyes. Considering different perspectives of a conflict can open up one's mind, foster empathy, and help the conflicting parties find a middle point at which to meet. Using the **Masks** worksheet found on page 34, have students create self-portraits in mask form. Store the masks in a secure place in the classroom to use as tools when conflicts arise.

When students encounter conflict, they exchange masks. With the masks held in front of their faces, students take turns stating the problem as the other person sees it.

When all parties have spoken, they put the masks aside. Then each person states how he or she is responsible for the problem. The class and the students in conflict brainstorm solutions and choose a solution that satisfies both.

A good resource about conflict resolution and peacemaking is *Learning the Skills of Peacemaking*, by Naomi Drew (Jalmar Press, 1987).

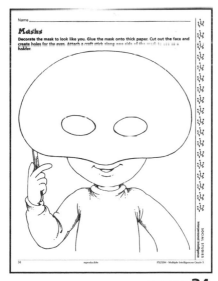

page 34

Water Rationing

In many parts of the world, safe water is a rare commodity. What would happen if safe drinking water became scarce in your community? Ask students to imagine that your community's main water source has become contaminated and have them work individually or with partners to determine a system for rationing water if they were to face this crisis. How is the water currently being used? How would water be distributed? What should the water be used for? How much water does each person need for survival? How should sanitation issues be handled, such as showers or use of toilets? What uses of water should be immediately terminated? What are some ways to bring other sources of safe drinking water to your community? Ask students to devise a plan to present to the class. Encourage students to discuss the plans, and comment on innovative solutions. Then have students pool their ideas as a class to create a final water-rationing plan.

Plan a Project

When studying about world governments, have students work on their cooperative group skills. Divide the class into groups of four and assign each group a type of government to research, such as a democracy, a monarchy, a dictatorship, or a meritocracy. Ask students to determine the kinds of information they want to discover and how they will divide the work. For example, after listing a series of questions they have about the government they are studying, group members might decide to have two people use reference books and two use the Internet. Also, have students decide how to present the information they gather. Do they want to create a group report, an oral presentation, a skit, or a class display? Praise your students for their group efforts.

Intrapersonal Intelligence

Pioneer Journal

Students can express their knowledge of pioneer days by using journal entries. Throughout your study of the pioneers, ask students to imagine that they live during these times. Ask students to ponder the following questions:

- What are your daily activities?
- Do you attend school or study in any way?
- What things do you do for enjoyment?
- Where do you live and what is your home like?
- What would a typical meal be?
- How do you feel about your life?
- What are your concerns?
- What are your hopes and dreams?

Periodically throughout the unit, have students write journal entries as if they actually live during the pioneer days. Remind students to express their feelings, thoughts, hopes, and concerns, as well as daily activities and chores. If students so desire, allow them to share journal entries with classmates.

Goal Setting

At the beginning of a new unit of study, encourage students to set personal goals for their own learning. Discuss the kinds of goals they may want to consider: to learn something specific; to read three good books about the topic; to finish a project within the given time frame; to work cooperatively in a group; and so on. Have each student record his or her goal on a slip of paper. Then ask them to put the papers in a safe place. At the end of the unit, have students review their goals and reflect upon whether or not they were achieved. Encourage students to share their reflections if they wish.

Naturalist Intelligence

The Survival Game

Arrange students into groups of three and have members of each group count off from 1 to 3. Ask them to imagine the following scenario:

You are hikers traveling together in a wilderness area and you have become lost. It is late autumn—the nights are cold, but there hasn't yet been snow. The nearest town is at least a two-day walk, and there are no public roads until you reach that town. You are all wearing jeans, sweatshirts, heavy socks and hiking boots. In addition, each of you has the following:

Person 1	Person 2	Person 3
lighter	bag of raisins	jackknife
8-foot length of rope	ball of heavy twine	heavy wool blanket
compass	6 dried apples	pocket calculator
large plastic bag	mechanical pencil	several rubber bands

Have each group meet to discuss its survival plan. Using only what they have with them and what they can find in nature, how will they keep themselves warm, fed, and safe from predators? How will they find their way to safety? Then ask groups to share their plans with the rest of the class. Have them reflect on how they had to cooperate and whether any conflicts arose. Ask groups which items were most essential to their survival plan and whether any items were worthless to them.

In the News

Read a news article provided by your teacher. Write down the title and important points of the article. Then rewrite the article in your own words.

Title of the original article:

_____

Important details:

_____

_____

_____

_____

_____

_____

_____

My Article

Title : _____

_____

_____

_____

_____

_____

_____

_____

_____

_____

_____

_____

_____

_____

SOCIAL STUDIES Verbal-Linguistic Intelligence

Name _____

The Great Debate

Use this activity sheet to help you plan your debate.

Debate Question: _____
_____

My View: _____

Important Points to Debate:

_____
_____
_____
_____
_____
_____
_____

Opponent's View: _____

Opponent's Possible Debate Points:

_____
_____
_____
_____
_____
_____

My Counterpoints:

_____
_____
_____
_____
_____

SOCIAL STUDIES

Verbal-Linguistic Intelligence

Masks

Decorate the mask to look like you. Glue the mask onto thick paper. Cut out the face and create holes for the eyes. Attach a craft stick along one side of the mask to use as a holder.

reproducible

SOCIAL STUDIES
Interpersonal Intelligence

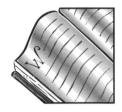

Verbal-Linguistic Intelligence

Word Problems

Read the entertaining story *Moira's Birthday,* by Robert Munsch (Annick Press, 1987), to your students. Ask them to pay attention to the number of children, pizzas, and cakes mentioned in the story. After reading the story, pose the following questions to students:

- If ten pizzas were first delivered to Moira's house and each pizza consisted of eight slices, how much pizza would each of the 200 kids have had to eat? (Answer: 4/10 of a slice)

- After the 200 children went home, the pizza deliverer brought 190 more pizzas. Each pizza consisted of eight slices. If Moira and her parents each ate three slices of pizza per day, how long would it take for them to eat all of the pizzas? (Answer: almost 169 days or just over five and a half months)

Have students pair up. Each student should create a word problem based on the book, exchange it with the partner, and solve the partner's problem.

Prefixes: Mathematically Speaking

Knowing common math-related prefixes can help students understand the meanings of words. On the chalkboard, write each of the prefixes listed below.

(1) uni-	(4) quad-	(7) sept- (100) centi-
(2) du- or bi-	(5) quint-	(8) octa- or octo-
(3) tri-	(6) sex-	(10) dec-

Invite students to use the meanings of the prefixes to help them answer questions you pose. Or write questions on index cards, with answers on the back, and display in the classroom as an independent activity. Sample questions are listed below.

- How many babies are in a set of sextuplets? Quintuplets? Triplets?
- How many musical notes are in an octave?
- How many wheels are on a unicycle? A bicycle? A tricycle?
- In how many events would you compete in a decathlon? A triathlon? A biathlon?
- How many cents are in a dollar?
- How many horns did triceratops have?
- How many years are in a century?

- How many legs does a quadruped have? A biped? An octopus?

- If a town is celebrating its centennial, how old is it?

- How many sides and angles are there in a triangle? A quadrilateral? An octagon? A decagon?

- How many people sing in a duet? A trio? An octet?

- How many years are there in a century?

- If you're bilingual, how many languages do you speak? If you're trilingual?

- How many sets of three zeros are there in a billion? A septillion?

- If you work in a triad, how many people are in your group?

- How many eyes do you use to look through binoculars?

- How many years are in a decade?

- How many decades has an octogenarian lived?

- How many centimeters are in a meter?

Note to the teacher: Students may ask about a prefix for the number nine. Explain that the prefix *non-* can mean *nine*. However, it usually means *not*. If students are interested, some examples of *non-* as a number prefix are: *nonagon* (figure with nine sides and angles) and nonet (nine voices or instruments).

Logical-Mathematical Intelligence

Number Fun

1. Choose any number

2. Add 3

3. Multiply by 2

4. Add 4

5. Divide by 2

6. Subtract the original number

Do this activity several times, always starting with a different number. What did you discover? The answer will be the same every time.

I Wonder...

With this activity, students come up with their own problems to solve based on their immediate world. Encourage students to ask mathematical questions that they can solve. For example:

- I wonder how many bricks it took to build our school.
- How much money do students pay for lunch every day in the cafeteria?
- Based on the number of students who are late to school each day, how many late passes do secretaries have to write every month/year?

Have students determine what they need to do or information they need to gather in order to solve each problem. Then have them acquire the information and solve the problem. Invite classmates to check each other's strategies and solutions when finished.

Calculator Messages

Here's a motivating way to have students practice using a calculator. Begin by printing the equations below on the blackboard for your students. By correctly entering each equation into a calculator and then turning it upside down, a word message appears. Have students try some of these equations and then make some of their own.

(The first equation is simply a series of numbers to be keyed in. Note the decimal point should be input before the numbers. This way the 0 is retained in the number. The rest of the list is equations.)

- .7734 spells hello
- $7 + 1 + 3 + 3 = hi$
- $1198.6 \times 5 = eggs$
- $44304 \div 8 = bess$
- $529 + 4,620 + 359 = boss$
- $401,336 \div 52 = bill$
- $972 - 36 - 18 = big$

Translation for upside down letters:

1 = lowercase i

3 = uppercase E

4 = lowercase h

5 = uppercase S

6 = lowercase g

7 = uppercase L

8 = uppercase B

9 = lowercase b or uppercase G

Working in Order

Review the concept of order of operations with students. Write the following equation on the chalkboard: $6 + 3 \times 2 = n$. Ask a volunteer to solve the equation.

Then ask the student to explain the steps he or she took to solve the problem. Place parentheses to show the first operation the student completed. For example, if the student says, "First I added 6 and 3," you would draw parentheses around the first two numbers: $(6 + 3) \times 2 = 18$.

Now rewrite the problem, placing the parentheses around the other pair of

page 44

page 45

numbers, i.e., 6 + (3 x 2). Ask students to solve the equation again and compare their solution to the first one. What made the difference?

Point out that when working with equations that involve a combination of operations, order does matter. Operations grouped in parentheses should always be solved first. If necessary, use another equation as an example, grouping the numbers in two different ways.

$$(12 \div 4) - (2 \times 1) = n$$

$$12 \div (4 - 2) \times 1 = n$$

Offer each student a copy of the **Mystery Equations** reproducible provided on page 44. Have them add parentheses to group the numbers in such a way that each equation is true.

Bodily-Kinesthetic Intelligence

Cooking

Ask students to write out one of their favorite family recipes. Supply index cards for this homework assignment. The next day, have students share what their recipe is with the rest of the class. For a lesson in fractions and measurement, each student should rewrite the recipe but double the amounts so that it serves twice as many people. Next they should half the original recipe. Make measuring cups and spoons available for this project to help students visualize the amounts.

Distribute the **Cooking Equivalents** worksheet on page 45 for the students to consult as they're converting. Have them use the standard cooking measurement abbreviations that are also supplied on the worksheet.

Compile the recipes in a class cookbook that can be used as a present. And, of course, have students volunteer to bring in some of the recipe dishes to class to share.

Body Angles

Have a quick review of angles, using arms instead of pencils. Ask students to stand far enough apart so they can stretch out their arms to the fullest. Then ask them to create a variety of angles using only their arms. For example, a right angle (90°) would be formed by holding the arm straight out from the shoulder and bent at the elbow with the hand pointing up. To form an obtuse angle (greater than 90°), the students would keep the upper arm steady and move the lower arms down. To form an acute angle (less than 90°), they would move the lower arm toward the shoulder. And a straight angle (180°) would be formed by stretching the arm straight out at shoulder height.

Visual-Spatial Intelligence

Litter Logic

This activity will challenge students to use their critical thinking skills. Give each student a copy of the worksheet on page 46, **Catch the Cat.** Then explain to them that they will have to look carefully at each of the cats and use the clues to determine the name of each cat. Through process of elimination, they should be able to determine which name belongs to each cat. This may take some time for students. You may want to allow them to work in cooperative groups if you think they would benefit from other students' help.

Visual Statistics

Who is the typical fifth grader? What is her or his shoe size? Favorite pizza topping? Best school subject? Most highly recommended book? Find out by conducting a survey. Working in investigation teams of two, each team chooses a different survey question. Establish a time for the teams to poll each other. Extend the investigation to include other fifth grade classes at school. Teams should compile answers and make a graph to visually present their findings—bar graphs, line graphs, circle graphs, or picture graphs. Have teams give oral reports and display their graphs. The class can also compile and post the survey results.

Toothpick Transformations

Here is another fun yet challenging activity. Each student will need six toothpicks. Distribute the worksheet on page 47, **Toothpick Transformations,** on which there are six toothpick figures. They are asked to move a certain number of the toothpicks in order to make the second figure. You may want to allow students to work in groups on this activity. As an extension, ask students to come up with toothpick transformations of their own to challenge their friends.

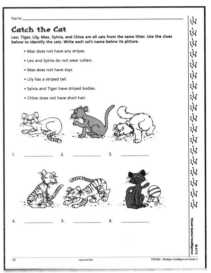

page 46

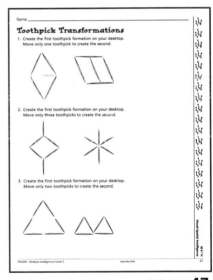

page 47

Musical Intelligence

Musical Fractions

Sheet music becomes interesting math work with this activity. Provide students with various pieces of sheet music. Discuss the time value of the

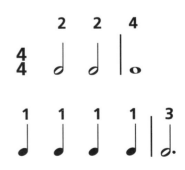

notes on the page, such as whole notes, half notes, quarter notes, eighth notes, etc. Then have each student begin with the first line of music. The purpose of the activity is to add up the fractional values of the notes on the line and arrive at a total fractional value for that line. Students who are able to read music should act as tutors throughout the activity for those students who are not familiar with reading music. Children continue with each line of the music in the same manner. When students have completed a page of music, have them work with partners to check each other's work. Hint: You may want to begin the activity with very simple pieces of music and move to more difficult pieces as students are ready for a greater challenge.

Musical Beats

Musical beats and brainpower combine to make this a fun activity. Have students select a piece of music to listen to in class. Ask students to count the number of beats they hear in the first 15 seconds of the song. Then, based on the length of the song (this can usually be found on the jacket of the CD or cassette tape), have students calculate the total number of beats in the song. After students have tried this a few times, have them listen to a song and guess the number of beats before calculating.

Interpersonal Intelligence

Classroom Statistics

Students themselves are filled with math possibilities! Have students solve the following problems, then come up with some of their own.

- Work in pairs to measure your height. Mentally estimate the total height of the class based on the number of students in the class and the two measurements taken.

- What is the average height of the students in your class? You may survey students in order to solve the problem.

- What is the total age in years of the students in your class? Solve mentally.

- What is the total number of family members for the entire class? You may survey one another before solving.

- What is the average number of members per family in the class?

Cooperative Problem Solving

Divide your students into groups of four. Assign each student a role to play, based on the role descriptions below. Then present students with a word problem dealing with a chosen skill. Students should work together to arrive at a solution. When the group problem-solving process is complete, have students share their feelings about working with the group and acting in their roles.

Reader/Announcer—This student reads the question to the group and also explains the group's problem-solving process to the whole class after solving.

Writer—This student uses paper and pencil to record the group's calculations.

Questioner—This student is responsible for questioning the group's strategies throughout the problem-solving process. The questioner might ask questions such as, "What information do we need to know in order to solve the problem?" or "What materials should we use to solve it?" and "Should we figure out a way to check our answer?"

Encourager—This student's job is to keep the group working by providing positive feedback for each student's participation. This student should complement useful suggestions made by others and also praise the whole group by making encouraging comments such as, "We're doing great! Let's keep working."

Peer Tutors

Most students find that their math skills are stronger in certain areas than in others. Give your students the chance to learn from one another and assist their peers as well. Display a sign-up sheet on a wall in your classroom. Have students list the math skills with which they feel confident enough to tutor others. Encourage all students to evaluate their own math skills and determine areas where they might benefit from some extra assistance. Urge students to seek out peer tutors when needed to receive math assistance.

How Did You Solve It?

Help students discover different ways to solve the same problem with this partner activity. Dictate a multiple-step word problem to your class. Have each child solve the problem using a chosen strategy such as manipulatives, drawing an illustration, or drawing a chart or table. After solving the problem, have students sit with partners to discuss their strategies. Ask students to compare their problem-solving methods. Were they the same or different? Did they learn any new strategies or helpful problem-solving methods?

Chocolate Chips

Just how many chips are in an entire bag of chocolate chip cookies? Divide students into groups of three or four. Give each group a bag of store-bought chocolate chip cookies. Students should discuss the best way to estimate the total number of chips in the bag. Students may break the cookies apart if necessary, but remind them not to eat them as they work! Ask students if it is necessary to count the chips in every cookie or if there is a way to closely estimate the total. Are there many ways to solve this problem or is there just one? When students have reached a conclusion, have them share their

answers with the class. Students may also be interested in finding out if other brands of cookies contain more or less chips per bag. After students have discussed their problem-solving processes, it's time to eat!

Intrapersonal Intelligence

Living on Your Own

Students will be surprised to find out the cost of living on their own in this activity. Have students list the basic necessary expense categories, such as food, rent, and utilities. Then have students use newspapers, apartment-finder guides, grocery store ads, and interviews with adults to determine the monthly costs for each category. Students combine the totals of each category to arrive at their grand totals. Extend the activity by asking students to brainstorm other needs, such as clothing, entertainment, transportation, insurance, etc. Have them research to determine the monthly costs for each item and add these amounts to the total. And finally, have students figure out the salary needed in order to support their expenses.

Math in Your Life

Encourage students to keep personal math journals. Each student should have a small spiral bound notebook to use. Or journals can be created by stapling sheets of lined paper between covers made from wallpaper or construction paper. Several times a week, have students write entries. Their writing can focus on how they use math in their daily lives, or students can reflect on what they have learned in math class. Other topics could be: how students feel about getting lower marks on tests than they had hoped, study schedules, how they feel about their successes.

Naturalist Intelligence

Geometry Scavenger Hunt

Arrange students into pairs or small groups and send them on a Geometry Scavenger Hunt. Set the boundaries of the search area according to your circumstances: the classroom only, several different areas in the school, the entire school, the outside play area, etc. Then provide each group with a list of items to be found. Suggestions are included at the end of this activity. Vary your list according to terms taught and items available in the search area.

Explain that groups must stay together as they search. They should check off any items they find, and for each they must record where the item was spotted. These records must be specific. For example, it isn't enough to say that an acute angle was spotted on the clock. The explanation should say that the hands of the clock at 1:10 formed an acute angle.

Set a time limit for the search. When the time is up, gather the groups together and see how many items were found by each group. Spot-check accuracy by asking each group to share what they wrote about several of its finds.

Search for...

circle	right angle	cylinder
square	acute angle	horizontal line
rectangle	obtuse angle	vertical line
hexagon	semicircle	polygon with 2 acute angles
octagon	oval	
triangle	set of parallel lines	cone
equilateral triangle	pyramid	cube
		set of perpendicular lines

Weather Patterns

Have students keep track of the weather over a period of at least three weeks. Collect data about precipitation, extent and type of cloud cover, high and low temperatures, and wind speed and direction. Data can be a combination of observation, measurement, and use of published or broadcast weather reports. Keep track of the information on a class-sized weather chart.

At the end of the time period, have students study the data they collected to see if there are any patterns revealed. Did the air temperature seem to be affected by precipitation or the amount of cloud cover? Were specific cloud formations associated with specific weather phenomenon? Did wind direction appear to have anything to do with precipitation? Discuss the students' observations.

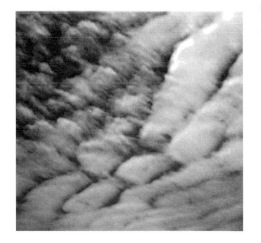

Mystery Equations

The equations below are all missing something important. The numbers aren't grouped! Add parentheses to show how you would have to group numbers to get the correct answer. Check your work by writing the equation on the line at the right, completing the work in parentheses.

Example: 400 ÷ 10 + 10 = 50

Answer: (400 ÷ 10) + 10 = 50 _____ 40 + 10 = 50

a. 24 ÷ 3 −1 = 7 _____

b. 65 − 2 x 6 = 53 _____

c. 400 ÷ 8 x 5 = 10 _____

d. 103 + 23 − 100 = 26 _____

e. 6 x 2 + 4 = 36 _____

f. 22 + 101 x 0 = 0 _____

g. 42 ÷ 7 + 21 ÷ 3 = 13 _____

h. 6 x 0 + 12 x 3 = 36 _____

i. 4 + 4 + 6 x 6 = 44 _____

j. 6 ÷ 3 + 6 − 3 + 6 + 3 = 14 _____

k. 100 ÷ 10 x 50 ÷ 10 = 50 _____

l. 3 x 4 + 5 + 6 + 8 − 7 = 24 _____

Now make up some mystery equations of your own. Each equation should be missing the parentheses. Ask a friend to group the numbers so the equation can be solved correctly. (And be sure that it can be!)

m. _____

n. _____

o. _____

MATH Logical-Mathematical Intelligence

Cooking Equivalents

Equivalent measurements can be used to convert your recipe to double the amount and half the amount. Convert your recipe using the measurement abbreviations listed below.

Common Kitchen Measurements

pinch (a few grains) = less than 1/8 teaspoon

2 tablespoons = 1 fluid ounce

5 tablespoons + 1 teaspoon = 1/3 cup

1 cup = 1/2 pint or 8 fluid ounces

2 pints = 1 quart

2 dry pints = 1 dry quart

4 pecks = 1 bushel

3 teaspoons = 1 tablespoon

4 tablespoons = 1/4 cup

16 tablespoons = 1 cup

2 cups = 1 pint

4 quarts = 1 gallon

8 dry quarts = 1 peck

Cooking Measurement Abbreviations

teaspoon—tsp.

tablespoon—tbsp.

ounce—oz.

fluid ounce—fl. oz.

pint—pt.

pound—lb.

quart—qt.

degrees Fahrenheit—°F

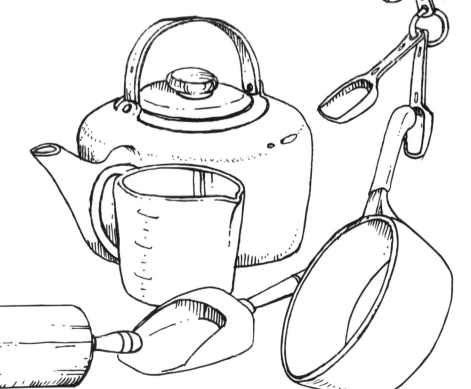

MATH
Bodily-Kinesthetic Intelligence

Catch the Cat

Leo, Tiger, Lily, Max, Sylvia, and Chloe are all cats from the same litter. Use the clues below to identify the cats. Write each cat's name below its picture.

- Max does not have any stripes.

- Leo and Sylvia do not wear collars.

- Max does not have toys.

- Lily has a striped tail.

- Sylvia and Tiger have striped bodies.

- Chloe does not have short hair.

1. _____ 2. _____ 3. _____

4. _____ 5. _____ 6. _____

reproducible

MATH
Visual-Spatial Intelligence

Toothpick Transformations

1. Create the first toothpick formation on your desktop.
   Move only one toothpick to create the second.

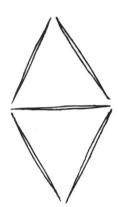 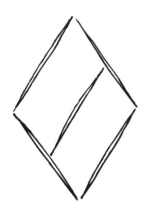

2. Create the first toothpick formation on your desktop.
   Move only three toothpicks to create the second.

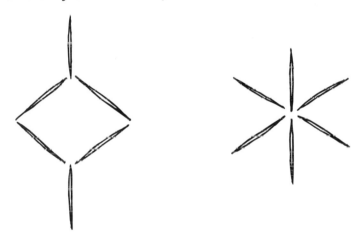

3. Create the first toothpick formation on your desktop.
   Move only two toothpicks to create the second.

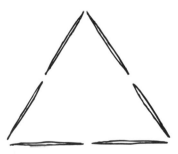 

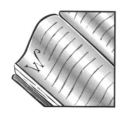

Verbal-Linguistic Intelligence

Science Heroes

Set up a display of biographies and autobiographies of scientists. Encourage students to select one scientist they would like to learn more about. Ask students to share what they learn about the scientist in the form of a poster. The poster should give the scientist's name, scientific specialty, nationality, and birth date. It should also list a few facts about the person's life and a summary of scientific achievements. Display the posters in the classroom as a Gallery of Science Heroes.

Some appropriate titles are listed below. Consult with your community or school librarian to find others.

- *Black Pioneers of Science and Invention,* by Louis Haber (Harcourt Brace, 1993)
- *The First Woman Doctor,* by Rachel Baker, a biography of Elizabeth Blackwell (Scholastic, 1987)
- *Marie Curie,* by Louis Sabin (Troll, 1985)
- *My Life With the Chimpanzees,* by Jane Goodall (PB Publishing, 1988)
- *Leonardo da Vinci,* by Norman F. Marshall (Silver Burdett, 1980)
- *Rachel Carson: Pioneer of Ecology,* by Kathleen Kudlinski (Puffin, 1989)
- *Thomas Alva Edison,* by Louis Sabin (Troll, 1983)
- *The Wright Brothers at Kitty Hawk,* by Donald J. Sobol (Scholastic, 1987)

Science Analogies

Review the use of analogies with students. Write the following example on the chalkboard: A tennis ball goes with a racket in the same way that a baseball goes with a _____. Ask students if they can fill in the missing word (bat). Discuss how they determined the answer. Help them understand that to solve the problem they need to identify the relationship of the first two terms (a tennis ball is used with or hit by a racket) and then think of a word that goes with baseball in the same way.

Show students how the sentence below would be written as an analogy:

tennis ball : racket as baseball : bat

Point out that identifying the relationships within an analogy means knowing something about the terms being used. Explain that they can use what they know about science to solve the following analogy:

water : liquid as oxygen : _____

Ask them to identify the relationship between the first two words. (Water is an example of a liquid.) Then have them identify the missing word and explain how the relationship between the first two words helped them determine the answer. (What is oxygen an example of? A gas.)Provide students with copies of the **Science Analogies** worksheet found on page 56. Have them complete the analogies and explain their thinking in determining the answers.

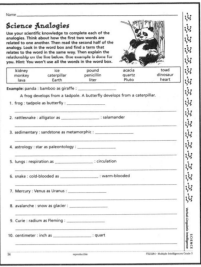

page 56

Campaign for Endangered Animals

Motivate your students to change the world with this activity. As a class, create a list of animals that are endangered, such as the California condor, the East African black rhinoceros, and the koala bear. Have each student choose one of the animals to research. Research should include facts about the animal itself, the factors contributing to its decline, as well as the efforts being made to save it. After gathering the information, discuss with students ways that they can develop a campaign to communicate their findings to others in a way that would persuade them to take action. Students can write a persuasive speech, create posters, pamphlets, videos, murals, etc., to share with classmates, other classes in the school, and parents.

Science in the News

Keep up to date on the latest information in science and technology with this activity. Create a bulletin board entitled "Science News." Then ask students to find newspaper and magazine articles about interesting science and technology topics. As students bring these articles to class, ask them to share them with classmates, write short summaries including their opinions and questions about the news, and then attach them to the class bulletin board for display.

Logical-Mathematical Intelligence

Time to Experiment

Discuss with students the steps in the scientific process. A simple explanation of the process is at right:

Discuss the idea that responsible scientists rely on the scientific method. Their hypotheses aren't always correct, but any experiment gives a scientist additional factual information to use when developing a new hypothesis.

Invite students to practice using the scientific method themselves as they design and carry out experiments. Remind them that a well-designed experiment uses a "control." A control is a parallel experiment that is exactly the same except for one factor. For example, an experiment to see how sunlight affects a bean plant would use two identical plants. They would be

1. **Identify a problem or question.**

2. **Formulate a hypothesis: a logical guess based on the known facts.**

3. **Design an experiment to test the hypothesis.**

4. **Carry out the experiment, observing and recording the results.**

5. **Draw conclusions based on the results of the experiments.**

page 57

treated exactly the same way except for the amount of sunlight they receive.

Offer students copies of the **Experiment Time** worksheet provided on page 57. Ask them to record information about their experiments on the worksheet. As they conduct their experiments, they should record observations and conclusions on the form as well. The list below suggests some problems students may want to investigate.

- Does an object's shape affect its ability to float?
- Does the surface on which a ball rolls affect its speed?
- Does distance affect the speed at which an object drops?
- Does water weigh more in its frozen state than in its liquid state?
- What kind of soil absorbs the most water?

Rainforest Riddles

For this project, each student chooses a rainforest animal to research. Students use factual books, encyclopedias, and other resources to find as many interesting facts about their animals as they can. Then each student writes a riddle incorporating several of the facts. Encourage students to choose at least one fact that will "give away" the identity of the animal. Allow students to share their rainforest riddles with classmates. Review the following example.

I live on the forest floor.

I am a good hunter.

I have spots.

I am in the cat family.

What am I?

(Answer: I am a jaguar.)

Design a Garden

Students can learn so much by having their own vegetable or flower garden. Before planting, have students plan the layout of the garden. First, decide on how many types of plants to grow and in what proportion—1/2 sunflowers, 1/3 tomatoes, etc. Students should then measure the size of the garden plot. Next they should determine the amount of space each plant will need in order to grow properly. This information can be found on seed packs or in gardening guides. Based on the amount of space each plant needs, have students calculate the number of plants that can be grown in each row of the garden and the number of rows that will fit in the designated space. Have each student draw a diagram of the garden before beginning to plant the seeds.

Bodily-Kinesthetic Intelligence

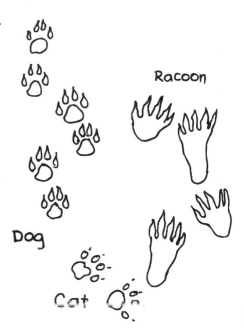

Racoon

Dog

Cat

Make Animal Tracks

Ask each student to choose an animal and research what its tracks look like. Don't forget animals such as dinosaurs, snakes, and those that drag their tail. Students should note that front tracks of animals are often different than hind tracks. A good reference for tracks is *Secrets of a Wildlife Watcher,* by Jim Arnosky (Beech Tree, 1991). Have students make tracks on long pieces of paper.

Track stamps can be made with a raw potato. Draw the track on the potato half and cut away the excess potato until the track protrudes about a quarter inch. This can be inked and used as a stamp.

Each student should label his or her track. The finished products can be attached to each other and hung in the classroom for display. Drawings of leaves, rocks, flowers, etc., can be added to the track mural to make it more lifelike and decorative.

How Acidic Is Your Rain Water?

When studying pollution, have students test the level of acid in your rain water. To do this, each student needs to create a container to catch the water. Before beginning, have students think about the best kind of container to use. Should the opening be large or small? How is it possible to avoid catching debris as well as rain water? Have students obtain rain containers and place them outside when rain is in the forecast. Rain water can be tested for acid levels by using ph strips. Allow students to test other items to see if they are acidic, basic, or neutral. Test liquid can be made by boiling red cabbage in water. The liquid is placed in individual paper cups. Substances are poured into the cups in small amounts. Neutrals will not change the color of the liquids. Acids will turn the liquid pink, and bases will turn the liquid green. Students should use the worksheet on page 58, **Acid, Base, or Neutral?** to record results.

page 58

Altitude Model

Help your students learn about the different levels of altitude in your state. After researching the varying altitudes of your state, have students create altitude pyramids out of the newspaper dough recipe below. Have students create a pyramid or other formation with levels representing the different altitudes in your state. Decide on a proportion, such as 1 inch equals 500 feet, so that the pyramids are proportionate. Allow the formations to dry for several days. Then have students paint their models with each altitude a different color. Have students label each level with the altitude and a city within the state that is located at that altitude. Altitude pyramids can also be created to illustrate the size differences between well-known mountains such as Everest, Kilimanjaro, McKinley, etc. Tall buildings can also be represented.

Newspaper Dough Recipe:

newspaper

water

flour

Tear strips of newspaper and place them in a large bowl of water. Be sure that all of the newspaper strips are submerged. Allow them to sit overnight. In the morning, drain and squeeze most of the excess water from the newspaper strips. In another container, mix flour and water together to make paste. Begin to mix the flour paste and newspaper by squeezing and kneading the mixture. Soon the material will feel somewhat smooth and squishy. At this point, the dough is ready for shaping.

Visual-Spatial Intelligence

Moon Phases

This simple accordion bookmaking activity can help students visualize and remember the phases of the moon. Materials: One sheet of 8 1/2-by-11-inch white paper, markers or crayons, scissors, tape.

Directions:

1. Fold the paper down the middle lengthwise.

2. Open the paper up and refold it the opposite way. Fold it a second time.

3. Unfold the paper. There should now be eight sections when unfolded.

4. Cut the paper in half lengthwise on the fold and tape the two pieces together to form one long piece of paper.

5. Trace a circle in each one of the eight sections. Then number the boxes 1 through 8

6. Write *New Moon* in the first box. Completely color in this circle with a dark- colored crayon or marker.

7. Label the third box *First Quarter Moon* and color in the left half of the circle with the dark crayon.

8. Label the fifth box *Full Moon.* Color this circle yellow or leave white.

9. Label section 7 *Last Quarter Moon* and color the right half of the circle with the dark color.

Study the pattern and determine how to color and label the remaining sections. What labels will they have? (Waxing Crescent, Waxing Gibbous, Waning Gibbous, Waning Crescent.) Tape the ends of the finished strip together to form a complete circle.

Discussion questions:

- How long is one complete cycle of the moon? (A lunar month is 28 days.)

- Have you heard of a blue moon? What is it? (Two full moons in the same calendar month.) Does this happen often? Why or why not?

- Why don't you see a new moon?

- What happens during a lunar eclipse? (Flashlights and tennis balls can be used to explore these last two questions. See illustration at right.)

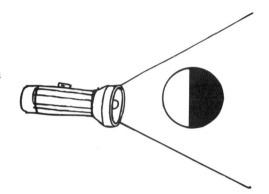

Constellation Projector

While studying astronomy have your students create their own Constellation Projector using an empty shoe box. Each student will need a shoe box, a sheet of black paper, and a pin to poke holes in the paper. One or two flashlights plus extra batteries should be available for the class to share.

1. Each student should pick the constellation she or he wants to create. With the pin, poke holes in the form of the constellation into the sheet of black paper. Make sure the constellation is slightly narrower than the narrow end of the shoebox.

2. Cut a rectangular slot into the top of the shoe box to hold the black paper. Cut another hole on the short end of the box that is slightly narrower than the piece of paper. A hole for a flashlight can be cut into the opposite end of the box if necessary.

3. With the lights off, project the image of the constellation on a light-colored wall. More than one constellation can be projected at one time if there is room in the classroom.

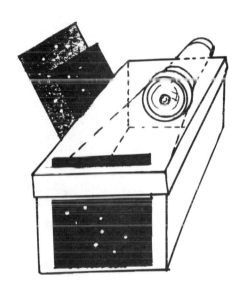

Creative Camouflage

Have students illustrate animal camouflage to learn about how animals thrive in their environment. Students should choose an animal that uses camouflage and write an essay about the habitat in which the animal lives, what it eats, if it lives in a herd or is solitary, how its young thrive, etc. Then have each student use colored pencils, crayons, markers, or paint to draw the camouflaged animal in its environment. Students can share their drawings with classmates to see if the hidden animals can be identified.

 Musical
Intelligence

Setting Nature to Music

Invite students to listen to and enjoy classical music with nature themes. Identify the name and composer of the piece. Then play a short selection from the larger work. Provide time for students to give their reactions, asking them to consider how the composer used music to represent nature. Were there passages that sounded like water or waves? Like wind or rain? Some appropriate compositions include:

· *La Mer,* by Claude Debussy

· *The Four Seasons,* by Antonio Vivaldi

· *Grand Canyon Suite,* by Ferde Grofé

· *The Water Music,* by George F. Handel

The Sound of Music

Review the concept that without vibration there is no sound. Ask students to think of musical instruments that are familiar to them and how each uses vibration to create its sound. When a guitar string is plucked, it vibrates. When you blow into a flute, the air vibrates. When a tambourine is shaken, all its parts vibrate. In each case, these vibrations travel through the air in the form of sound waves. The pitch, or frequency, of a sound depends on how long the sound waves are. The faster an object vibrates, the shorter the wavelength of the sound it makes. The shorter the wavelength, the higher the pitch is.

Invite students to experiment with sound and pitch by making simple "junk" instruments such as the following:

Shoe-box Strings: Cut an oval hole in the center of the lid of a shoe box. Replace the lid. Then stretch 7 rubber bands of different thicknesses around the shoe box the long way. Arrange the rubber bands from thinnest to thickest. Slide a pencil under the rubber bands at either end of the shoe box. Pluck on the strings to create sound. How does the pitch change as you move from the thickest to the thinnest string?

Bottle Woodwind: Make a row of seven glass bottles that are approximately the same size and shape. Pour a small amount of water into the first bottle. Then add water to the other bottles with each one having more water than the one before it. Create sound by blowing across the tops of the bottles. How does the pitch change as you move from the emptiest to the fullest bottle?

Junk Percussion: Make several sets of claves from sticks of varying thicknesses. For each set of claves, the two sticks should be about the same thickness. Try striking each set in turn, beginning with the thinnest. How does the pitch change from set to set?

Interpersonal
Intelligence

Human Body Game Board

This activity allows students to put their heads together to create a fun and informative game. Divide your class into groups of three or four students.

Explain to students that they will be creating a game board about the human body. In order to create the game, they will need to gather many facts about different parts of the body. Have students decide how they will gather information about the digestive system, the respiratory system, the skeleton, and the muscular system. Have students record their facts as they find them. When twenty or more facts are found, ask the groups to create a game board for their classmates to play. Each space on the board will have a question about the body that must be answered in order for students to progress through the game.

Intrapersonal Intelligence

Taste Experiments

We use our tongues to taste things that are sweet, salty, sour, and bitter. Do you know which part of the tongue can taste each of these? Sweet is tasted at the front of the tongue. Salt is tasted on the sides near the tip of the tongue. Sour is tasted along the side, and bitter at the back of the tongue.

Have students draw a diagram of the tongue and do the experiment below. As they complete the activity they should label their drawing of the tongue *sweet, salty, sour,* and *bitter* in the appropriate areas.

Provide students with several cotton swabs and three small cups filled with the following substances:

- sweet—sugar water
- salty—salt water
- sour—lemon juice
- bitter—strong coffee unsweetened

Students should be instructed to dip a cotton swab into a substance and then run it over different areas of the tongue to identify where it can be tasted. After testing each substance, have students mark their tongue drawing.

To extend the activity, explain to students that when they hold their noses they cut off the flow of air to their olfactory receptors (smelling sensors) inside the nose. This will dull their sense of taste. Tell students to work in pairs to test their dulled senses. Give each pair of students two slices of orange and two slices of grapefruit. Then challenge them to close their eyes and hold their nose while their partner feeds them a piece of fruit with a fork. They have to try to guess which piece of fruit is which. After all students have tried the experiment, discuss the results with the class.

Name _____

Science Analogies

Use your scientific knowledge to complete each of the analogies. Think about how the first two words are related to one another. Then read the second half of the analogy. Look in the word box and find a term that relates to the word in the same way. Then explain the relationship on the line below. One example is done for you. Hint: You won't use all the words in the word box.

kidney	ice	pound	acacia	toad
monkey	caterpillar	penicillin	quartz	dinosaur
lava	Earth	liter	Pluto	heart

Example: panda : bamboo as giraffe : _____

      A panda eats bamboo. A giraffe eats acacia.

1. frog : tadpole as butterfly : _____

_____

2. rattlesnake : alligator as _____ : salamander

_____

3. sedimentary : sandstone as metamorphic : _____

_____

4. astronomy : star as paleontology : _____

_____

5. lungs : respiration as _____ : circulation

_____

6. snake : cold-blooded as _____ : warm-blooded

_____

7. Mercury : Venus as Uranus : _____

_____

8. avalanche : snow as glacier : _____

_____

9. Curie : radium as Fleming : _____

_____

10. centimeter : inch as _____ : quart

_____

        reproducible

Name _____

Experiment Time

Use the form below to identify a problem, record a hypothesis, plan an experiment to test your hypothesis, record your observations, and come to some conclusions about how accurate your hypothesis was.

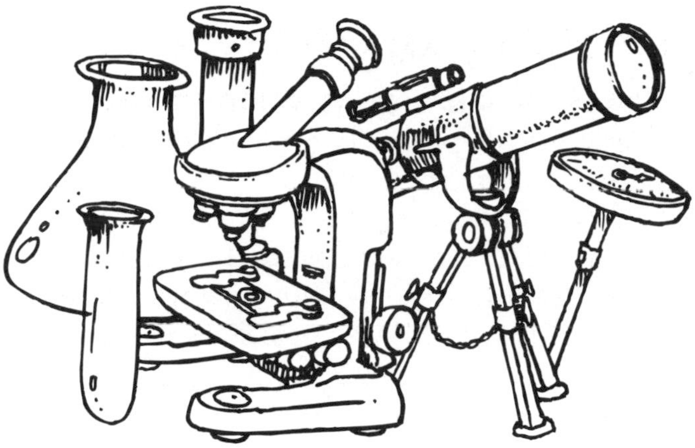

Problem or question:

_____

_____

Hypothesis: _____

_____

_____

Experiment Plan: _____

_____

_____

Materials Needed: _____

_____

_____

Procedure: _____

_____

_____

Observations: _____

_____

_____

Conclusions: _____

_____

_____

SCIENCE Logical-Mathematical Intelligence

Acid, Base, or Neutral?

Are the substances below acids, bases, or neutral? Use the chart below to record predictions and test results. Estimate what the pH level is based on the scale.

pH Scale

0. . . . . .7. 4
acid   neutral   base

Substance	Prediction	Color of Test Liquid	Acid, Base, or Neutral?	pH level
baking powder				
antacid tablet				
aspirin				
lemon juice				
water				
rubbing alcohol				
baking soda				

Reflections:

_____
_____
_____
_____
_____
_____
_____
_____
_____
_____

Verbal-Linguistic Intelligence

Masterpiece Masters

Expose your students to great works of art by famous artists. Provide students with books of artists' work or visit the web sites listed below and read about each artist. Have students write reports about their chosen artist.

> Cassatt, Cezanne, Gauguin, Homer, Manet, Monet, Munch, Picasso, Pissarro, Rembrandt, Renoir, Sisley, and Toulouse-Lautrec— http://lonestar.texas.net/~mharden/artchive/ (Once at this site, navigate to the desired artchive.)
>
> da Vinci—http://sunsite.unc.edu/wm/paint/auth/vinci
>
> Goya—http://www.imageone.com/goya/parasol.html
>
> Rembrandt—http://sunsite.unc.edu/wm/paint/auth/rembrandt/
>
> van Gogh—http://www.iem.ac.ru/wm/paint/auth/gogh

Logical-Mathematical Intelligence

Autobiographical Time Lines

Students in this activity create personal time lines that illustrate the important dates in their lives, such as their birth, first day of school, favorite vacations, encounters with memorable people, awards, jobs, births of siblings, deaths of loved ones, change of address or school, etc. Students can illustrate their time lines themselves or bring in photos and mementos. After bringing the time line up to the present, students can project the time line into the future and illustrate where they hope they'll be in the years to come.

Bodily-Kinesthetic Intelligence

Gesture Drawing

Explain to the class that gesture drawing is a drawing technique using

quickly drawn lines that create a sense of energy and motion. The object of the exercise is to draw as fast as possible to capture the energy of the subject. Each drawing is created in 60 seconds, and the pen should be moving continually within this time period, without leaving the paper.

Gesture Drawing Directions:

Materials: Construction paper, pen

1. Choose a volunteer to stand where she or he can be see by everyone in the class. The volunteer should strike a pose that conveys action, such as running, dancing, pitching a baseball, etc..

2. Have the students quickly draw the overall shape of the person. Their pens should never leave the paper as they draw. They are trying to draw an outline rather than capture details such as facial features, fingers, or hair.

3. Tell the students to start drawing faster. And even faster!

4. After one minute, their drawings are complete. Begin the procedure with a different model.

Creative Sculptures

Introduce your students to three-dimensional sculpture called Minimal Art. This type of sculpture, which consists of modular shapes, emerged in New York City in the 1960s. The work of Donald Judd, Robert Morris, and Tony Smith can be viewed by students at the web sites below. After observing these artistic structures, have students create their own geometric sculptures using a variety of materials such as wood, wire, or plastic bottle caps. Students may also try to create modular shapes from moldable material such as salt dough (see page 13 for the recipe).

Donald Judd—Art in Context web site

http://www.artincontext.com/listings/images/genre/minimal.htm

Robert Morris—The Sculpture Center: Ohio Outdoor Sculpture Inventory

http://www.sculpturecenter.org/$spindb.query.oosilist.oosiarti.Morris.Robert.155

Tony Smith—The Sculpture Center: Ohio Outdoor Sculpture Inventory

http://www.sculpturecenter.org/$spindb.query.oosilist.oosiarti.Smith.Tony.218

Frank Lloyd Wright

Give your students the opportunity to observe and analyze the modern architecture of Frank Lloyd Wright. Provide books of Wright's work or allow students to visit the web site below to view his commercial and residential designs. Ask students to identify the characteristics that make his work unique and what the philosophy behind some of his designs was. Then have students draw pictures or write an essay of their own dream house and why they designed it the way they did.

Frank Lloyd Wright Appreciation Site:

http://members.aol.com/ddukesf/index.html

Visual-Spatial Intelligence

The Art of Sand Painting

Sand painting, which today is considered by many to be a form of art, is actually a healing rite performed by many Southwestern Native-American tribes, including the Navajo and Pueblos. These paintings, made of pollen and other colorful, powdered materials, are designed on the ground and later destroyed when the healing rite is complete. Have students discover more information about Native-American sand painting and then create designs of their own. Sand can be colored with fabric dye or a sandlike material can be made by mixing salt with pulverized, colored chalk.

Students should first draw in pencil a design on tag board. To adhere the sand to the design, squeeze a trail of glue in a desired location, sprinkle sand on top of the glue, and gently shake off the excess. Students should continue in this manner until the pencil lines are covered. Allow the glue to dry completely before displaying.

Tissue-Paper Art

This project allows students to create designs with interesting blends of color. Provide each student with a sheet of white construction paper, assorted colors of tissue paper, a sponge, and water. Be sure that the tissue paper is the type that will bleed its color when wet. Students should wear smocks to protect clothing. Ask students to cut different colors of tissue paper in various shapes. Then, students should place each tissue piece on the art paper. Next students should gently presses a damp sponge on top of the tissue paper. The ink from the tissue paper will bleed onto the art paper. Finally, they can remove the tissue paper and discard it. Tell students to continue in this manner with different shapes and colors to create an interesting design. Suggest that students overlap the tissue paper colors for appealing effects.

Totem Poles

Native Americans of the Pacific Northwest are known for their totem wood carvings. Students can research these totems and even view interesting photographs by using library resources or an electronic encyclopedia such as Microsoft Encarta 97 Encyclopedia Deluxe Edition (Microsoft). After learning about totem poles, have students create a class totem pole. To do

this, each student needs a cylindrical cardboard oatmeal container, a 9-by-14-inch sheet of construction paper, glue, scissors, assorted colors of construction-paper scraps, and paint or markers.

To begin, students should cover the oatmeal container with the construction paper and glue. Three-dimensional features can be added to the tube and features can be drawn or painted as well, to create the totem face. When all students have completed their totems, stack totems on a tall rod such as a dowel or shower bar. To stack, cut holes in the top and bottom of the containers large enough for the rod. Prop the totem pole in a corner of your classroom for display. And encourage students to share why they designed their totems as they did.

Be an Artist

Your students can create works of art similar to those of artist Edvard Munch. Begin by having children observe some of Munch's work such as "The Scream." Look for an online collection of Munch's paintings at the following web site:

http://lonestar.texas.net/~mharden/artchive/ftptoc/munch/munch_top.html

Draw students' attention to the artist's use of wavy lines in his paintings. After students familiarize themselves with the paintings, have them create artwork similar to this style. To do this, each student needs a sheet of construction paper, liquid tempera paint in an assortment of colors, and a wide-toothed comb. To make the background of the picture, students should squeeze several colors of liquid tempera paint onto the paper. Next students should gently drag the comb through the paint in different directions to create wavy lines. Allow the background to dry overnight. Then students can paint a picture in the foreground to complete the work of art.

Musical Intelligence

Music on the Web

Students can learn a variety of musical facts by visiting musical web sites. Have partners work together to determine the types of musical information they would like to discover. Demonstrate how to conduct a search to find sites about music, instruments, composers, etc. Have students begin their Internet adventure by visiting the site below.

Berit's Best Music Sites for Children:

http://db.cochran.com/li_toc:theoPage.db

On this page students can access links to sites about electric guitars, drums, singers and songwriters, classical music, and much more. Have partners make note of interesting information found on the Internet to share.

All That Jazz

Celebrate a part of African-American history with this study of some great jazz musicians. Duplicate and distribute the **All That Jazz** reproducible on page 66 for each student. Then allow students to work with partners to search for information about the musicians using library resources, the Internet, or a computer program such as Microsoft Encarta 97 Encyclopedia (Microsoft). Students should solve the riddles and fill in the blanks on the worksheet when they match the musicians with the facts. Students can also collect interesting information that they find in their searches and create questions of their own to ask classmates. Be sure to have students listen to some jazz music as well.

Many jazz sound bytes are available in the Microsoft Encarta 97 Encyclopedia Deluxe Edition. Simply open the program and navigate to the encyclopedia articles section. Then, from the Find menu, scroll down to the musician's name and click. The featured jazz musicians on the student page include Ella Fitzgerald, Louis Armstrong, Count Basie, Dizzy Gillespie, Charlie Parker, Fats Waller, Lester Young, and Earl "Fatha" Hines. Most of these articles contain sound bytes as well as photographs and information that can be easily accessed.

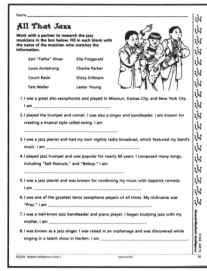

page 66

Interpersonal Intelligence

Color Wheel Mosaic

This art project will give students an opportunity to see the relationship of one color to another as they are positioned on a color wheel. In groups, students will create a mural-sized mosaic of the color wheel. Each student will be assigned a color and will create this portion of the mosaic.

Begin by displaying a large color wheel. Point out the primary colors–yellow, red, and blue–and secondary colors–orange, purple, and green. Explain that between these six colors are intermediate colors–yellow-orange, red-orange, red-violet, blue-violet, blue-green, and yellow-green. Complementary colors are colors that are found directly opposite each other on the wheel. Pairs of complementary colors are red and green, for example, and orange and blue.

Distribute **The Color Wheel** worksheet on page 67 to the class and have them color or paint the wheel with appropriate colors, trying to blend the colors together.

Before starting the project below, review the process of creating a mosaic with the class. Explain that historically mosaics were made with tile, stone, or glass pieces called tesserae. Display pictures of mosaics found in mosques, walls, or furniture. Jewelry and tile floors are also created with the mosaic technique.

page 67

Directions for a Color Wheel Mosaic

Materials: paper, watercolor, tempera paint, or crayons, glue, scissors, glitter glue (optional)

1. Draw a large circle on butcher paper. On the inside of the circle mark lightly with pencil the 12 sections of the color wheel. Put the color wheel on a table where it is accessible. (More than one color wheel may be necessary depending on the number of students in the class.)

2. Each student should choose a primary or secondary color of the wheel.

3. On white paper, students should draw a triangle the same size as a section of the color wheel. The paper should be colored with either crayons or paint before it is cut into small pieces. Each student will be creating a piece of the wheel, making sure that his or her color blends with the colors bordering it. Therefore, more than one color will be used by each student. For example, a student who chooses the color green will color his or her section green to yellow-green on one side, and green to blue-green on the other side.

4. Once the paper has been colored, it should be cut into small pieces.

5. Students can be working simultaneously to glue their tesserae to the wheel. Point out to students that they must leave room for other students to intersperse their tesserae around the borders of their colors so that the colors will blend nicely.

6. Glitter can be added to the finished spectrum.

Intrapersonal Intelligence

Creative Dreams

Ask students to reflect on their interests in the fine arts. Then have them decide whether they see themselves more as artists, writers, actors, musicians, or dancers. Have each student write a journal entry about his or her creative interests. To inspire the student's writing, list the questions below on the board.

- Am I an artist, a writer, an actor, a musician, or a dancer?

- If I could develop one of these talents, which would it be?

- How do I exhibit creative talent in my life today?

- What could I do in the future to pursue my creative goals and dreams?

- What would a typical day be like when I achieve this dream? Use first person and present tense to answer this question. Example: *I am tuning my guitar in the studio with the bass player.*

For inspiration in this activity read aloud *A Very Young Musician,* by Jill Krementz (Simon and Schuster, 1991). Or make the book available to interested students to read independently. This nonfiction book features a ten-year-old trumpet player. Another biography is *A Young Painter,* by Zheng Zhensun and Alice Low (Scholastic, 1991), which is about a gifted young painter in China.

Naturalist Intelligence

Crayon Resist Art Project

This project helps students appreciate water in the world around them, and as a medium with which to create. Explain that they will be studying the interaction of water and wax in a process called crayon resist. In this technique crayon is applied to paper and then covered with watercolor. The wax in the crayon will repel the water, so that the paint will not cover the crayon.

As a subject matter students should choose an image with water as its theme. Some suggestions are: a rainbow, an undersea picture, a surfer at the ocean, an aquarium, seashells on the shore.

Directions for Crayon-Resist project

Materials: Construction paper, crayons, watercolors, paintbrushes, pencils

1. With a pencil, lightly sketch your picture on a sheet of white construction paper.

2. Use light-colored crayons to trace the pencil marks. Press firmly with the crayon.

3. Paint over the crayon areas with watercolor using broad horizontal strokes. Make sure to load your brush with lots of watercolor to make the painting bright.

Note: Be sure to show the class how to rinse the brush with water before using a new color.

All That Jazz

Work with a partner to research the jazz musicians in the box below. Fill in each blank with the name of the musician who matches the information.

Earl "Fatha" Hines Ella Fitzgerald

Louis Armstrong   Charlie Parker

Count Basie   Dizzy Gillespie

Fats Waller   Lester Young

1. I was a great alto saxophonist and played in Missouri, Kansas City, and New York City.
   I am _____.

2. I played the trumpet and cornet. I was also a singer and bandleader. I am known for creating a musical style called swing. I am

   _____.

3. I was a jazz pianist and had my own nightly radio broadcast, which featured my band's music. I am _____.

4. I played jazz trumpet and was popular for nearly 60 years. I composed many songs, including "Salt Peanuts," and "Bebop." I am

   _____.

5. I was a jazz pianist and was known for combining my music with slapstick comedy.
   I am _____.

6. I was one of the greatest tenor saxophone players of all times. My nickname was "Prez." I am _____.

7. I was a well-know jazz bandleader and piano player. I began studying jazz with my mother. I am _____.

8. I was known as a jazz singer. I was raised in an orphanage and was discovered while singing in a talent show in Harlem. I am _____.

FINE ARTS
Musical Intelligence

The Color Wheel

Color or paint the colors in the color wheel.
Try to blend the colors where they meet.

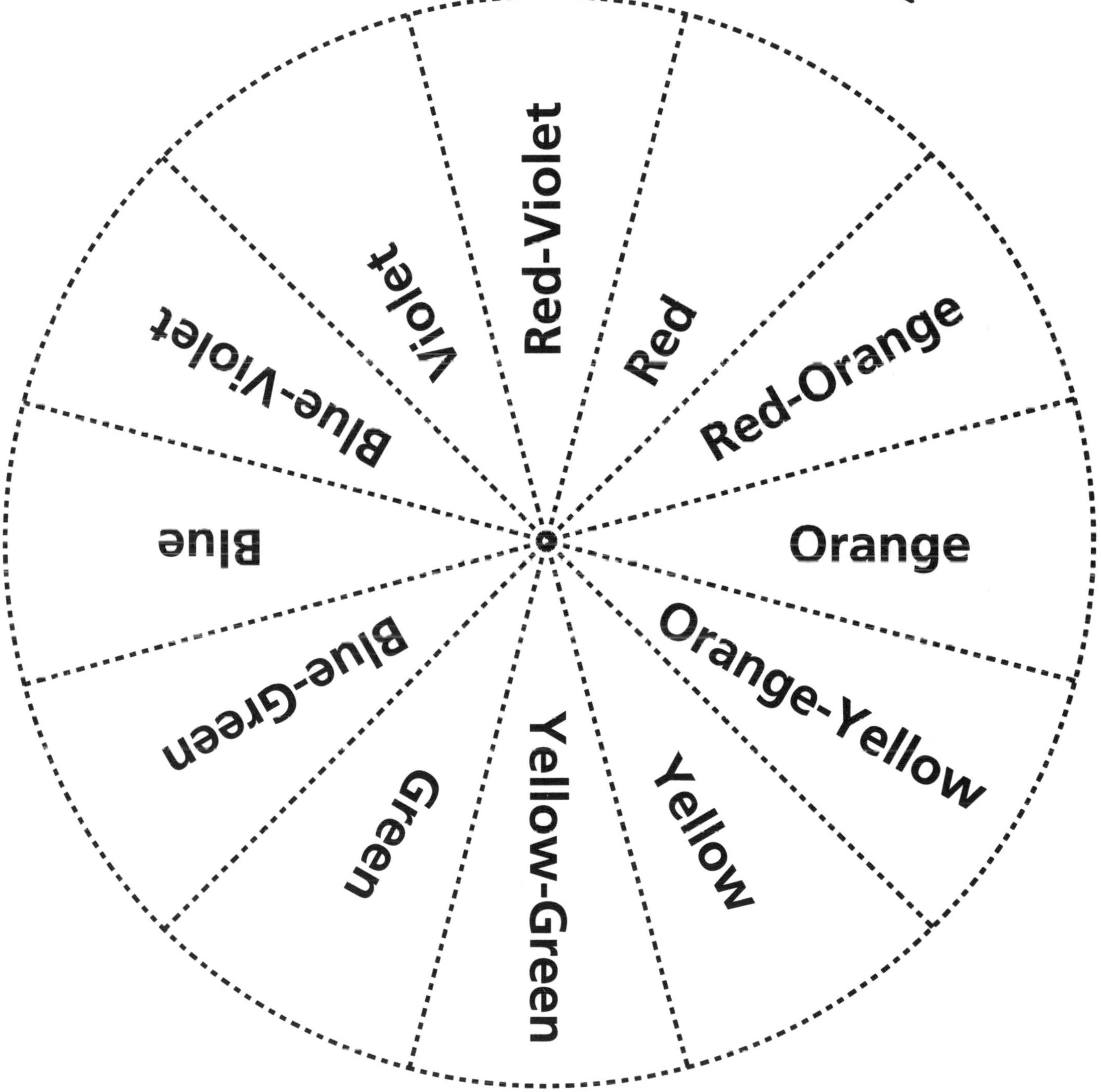

Red-Violet

Violet

Blue-Violet

Blue

Blue-Green

Green

Yellow-Green

Yellow

Orange-Yellow

Orange

Red-Orange

Red

FINE ARTS
Interpersonal Intelligence

Verbal-Linguistic Intelligence

Sports Reporting

Invite students to act as sports journalists by writing an account of a school or professional sporting event they attended or watched on television. Remind them that the article must offer the information required by any news article: answers to the questions *who, what, when, where, how,* and *why.* Encourage students to add colorful headlines that feature action words.

Famous Olympians

Have students select a famous Olympian. They can choose someone who has won a medal, or someone who has been a good sport and tried very hard but never won a medal. They should use whatever resources they have available to find out what they can about the Olympian. Encourage them to use print resources from the library, electronic resources such as an electronic encyclopedia, or the Internet. Two electronic encyclopedias are Encarta (Microsoft) or Compton's 1998 Interactive Encyclopedia (The Learning Company). Challenge students to find out the answers to the following questions about the athlete they are researching, and some of their own, and write a report.

- When did the athlete start playing the sport?

- How did he or she get interested in the sport?

- When did the athlete know he or she wanted to be in the Olympics?

- How was the athlete's childhood different from the average person's childhood?

- Who is his or her hero?

- What are the athlete's future plans?

Jump Rope Fun

Add some fun to jumping rope with this activity. Invite students to create chants to accompany their rope jumping. For inspiration, share with your students the book *Miss Mary Mack and Other Children's Street Rhymes,* by Joanna Cole and Stephanie Calmenson (William Morrow and Company, 1990), and have them read some playground chants and rhymes. Then encourage students to work individually or with others to create an original chant of their own. When chants are complete, ask students to memorize them so they can recite the chants while jumping rope on the playground. If desired, have students teach their chants to younger students in your school.

Logical-Mathematical Intelligence

A New Game

Have students work together in groups for this challenging activity. Provide students with a variety of physical education equipment. Be sure to include balls, bean bags, nets, cones, and anything else that students may have fun with. Explain to students that in their groups, they need to create a new game using the equipment you have provided. They need to establish rules for the game and perhaps a time limit. The game also needs a clear objective. Once they have decided what their game should be, they need to test it out within their groups. Are there any rules they left out? Any problems with the game they didn't consider? After the games are set, have students teach the games to each other.

Kickball Graphs

Have your class play a game of kickball. While children are playing, record statistics for the game such as runs scored per inning, individual student scores, runs "kicked in," etc. When the game ends, present the inning scores to students and have each student create a graph reflecting the information. Suggest that students choose types of graphs that will most clearly show the statistics. Students may make bar graphs, line graphs, pie graphs, or Venn diagrams. Encourage students to think of other information from the kickball game that could be reflected in the form of a graph.

Bodily-Kinesthetic Intelligence

Playtime Sports Preparation

Activities that involve throwing, catching, kicking, and running build skills that students need when playing organized sports. At recess time, try some of the skill-builder activities described below.

Ball Volley: Mark two parallel lines about 20 feet apart. Divide the class into two equal teams. Team members stand behind the line on their team's side, except for one player, who will act as the first server. The server tosses a volleyball up slightly with one hand and hits it with the other, sending it toward the opposite team. If a member of that team can catch the ball before it hits the ground, he or she becomes the server. Otherwise, the first server takes another turn. Keep score for each team. Continue for a specified length of time.

Hot Ball:. Players stand in a circle, facing inward. The designated starter places a soccer ball on the ground in front of him or her. The starter calls out, "Hot ball!" and kicks the ball across the circle, soccer style (using the inside of the foot). The player the ball is kicked toward quickly kicks the ball somewhere else. The object is to keep the "hot" ball moving as quickly as possible. Continue until the ball is kicked out of the circle. Then a new player can act as starter and set things in motion again.

Ball Rounds: Play this game on a hard surface. Have players form two equal teams, each with a designated leader. The teams form two large circles. Using both hands, the leader passes a basketball to the player on the right. As quickly as possible, the second player passes to the third, and so on until the ball returns to the leader. The leader then bounces the ball off the playground surface, toward the player on the right. That player catches the ball, then bounces it to the next person, who does the same. The game ends when the ball reaches the leader again. Check to see which team moves the ball fastest.

Play Paddle Ball

Students can create their own equipment for this paddle ball activity. To make a paddle or racket, provide each student with a wire coat hanger. The student should bend the triangular section of the hanger into a diamond shape. Then have the student stretch a nylon stocking over the diamond. The stocking is then trimmed and secured to the base of the diamond with a rubber band. To play, students paddle a foam ball or balloon back and forth to each other. Students may also try to just keep the ball from touching the ground.

Visual-Spatial Intelligence

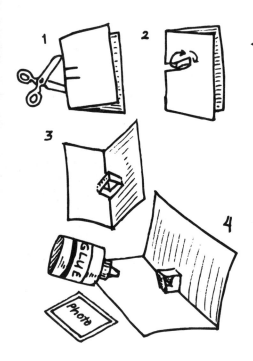

Pop-Ups

Take a photograph of each student participating in a sport. After the film is developed, help the students to make a pop-up card featuring their photographs. Give each student two sheets of colored construction paper and have him or her follow these directions to make the card:

1. Fold one sheet of construction paper in half.

2. Cut two half-inch slits from the fold near the center of the paper to make a tab. See illustration at left.

3. Unfold the paper and push out the tab.

4. Fold the second sheet of paper in half and glue it to the outside of the first sheet. Make sure you do not glue down the tab.

5. Write a special message in your card and decorate the front and inside.

6. Cut around your photograph so that only your image is left.

7. Glue your image to the tab and deliver your card to a family member or friend.

Musical-Rhythmic Intelligence

Set the Mood

Your students can set the mood for physical education classes with this activity. Break up the class into groups. First have groups select music that would be appropriate for warm-up exercises. You may suggest that students choose music that is lively and yet not too fast. Next have students choose several songs that would be motivating during a high-energy game or exercise time. Students should determine the length of time needed for the game or activity and select music that will play throughout this time. Finally, have students select music that would be appropriate for a cool-down period. Encourage students to choose music that is relaxing and peaceful. After students make their musical selections, have them play the songs in sequence and try out different kinds of exercises for the different kinds of music. Then have them use their musical sequences during physical education class.

Interpersonal Intelligence

Coaching

Hold a discussion about the role of coaches in sports. Talk about the importance of a coach's ability to communicate clearly and positively. Have students suggest ideas they have for positive comments.

Select a skill to practice, such as kicking a ball, dribbling a ball, or hitting a ball with the palm of the hand. Have pairs of students take turns acting as coach and athlete. The athlete will practice the skill as the coach will practice offering suggestions and positive comments. Follow-up the activity with a discussion about the coaching methods that were helpful and those that were not helpful.

Group Triathlon

The following three activities are for groups of students and require communication and cooperation. The activities can be timed and each considered a portion of a triathlon. Groups can compete against each other for a final prize. Make sure students are provided with opportunities to practice before the competition begins.

Group Seating

This event requires trust and working together. Have groups of students stand in a circle shoulder to shoulder. Tell them to make a quarter turn to the right and take a step sideways into the circle. Then tell them to bend their knees and sit. If everyone works together, each student will be sitting on another student's knees in the circle. If one person falls, all will fall. When the students can do this successfully, encourage them to make a "wave" with their arms, one student raising and lowering both arms at a time.

Untie the Knot

In a large, cleared area, ask groups of students to join hands with their group members to create a large knot of people. Students can cross arms above and below classmates' arms. They may also twist their bodies around and step over classmates' joined hands. When the knot is complete, students must work together to "untie" the knot without releasing hands at any time. Encourage students to move under and step over other students' hands. The goal is to end up with one large circle of students holding hands.

Up You Go!

Have each group create a human pyramid. Students can create the pyramid levels by crouching on their hands and knees. The base level should consist of four students on hands and knees. Have students in each group develop a strategy for building the pyramid and consider how those on the second and third levels will climb up. Be sure to choose "spotters" to help prevent injury. As groups successfully build their human pyramids, have them discuss ways to make the task easier and faster. Then have the groups build their pyramids again to improve their team skills and increase their times.

Intrapersonal Intelligence

Increase Your Time

Have students think about their ability to walk or run a mile. Ask them to time themselves as they cover the distance. Times can be recorded on the **Walking/Running Improvement Log** on page 74. As each student walks or runs, have him or her think about the pace and the ease at which he or she is moving. When finished, have students set goals for increasing the time and distance. Encourage students to increase the time and distance in small increments. A goal for each week should be determined and a plan for accomplishing the goal should be recorded. As students time the distance each week, have them reflect on progress made. Students should ask

page 74

questions such as:

- Am I experiencing any difficulties as I'm running/walking?
- Am I feeling tired at this pace?
- Could I move any faster and still be comfortable?
- Could I increase my endurance by increasing the number of days each week that I walk or run?

Encourage students to ask themselves these and other questions weekly and allow them to share their strategies with others.

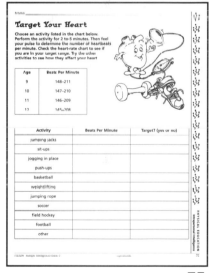

Food for Your Health

Does eating healthy really make a person feel better? Have students reflect on their eating habits with this activity. Each student should label a page in a notebook for each day of the week. The student should record the food he or she eats each day. At the end of the day, have students make reflections about headaches or body aches, feeling relaxed, nervous, tired, energetic, hungry, full, etc. Have each student write about how she or he felt on the page designated for that day. At the end of the week, ask students to compare the food eaten to the way they felt each day to see if any conclusions can be made. Does eating a well balanced diet make you feel better? Does eating too much of a certain food bring on headaches? Invite students to share their findings with others.

Heart Rate Activities

Challenge students to perform certain activities that will raise their heart rate. After they perform the activities listed on the worksheet on page 75, **Target Your Heart,** they should check their heart rates and record them on the same sheet. There is a chart at the top of the sheet that will help students to know if they are within their target heart rate.

Naturalist Intelligence

page 75

Outdoors Project

Students can create a personal project based on an outdoor activity that they enjoy doing on their own. Some activities to choose from are: hiking, fishing, camping, bird watching, cross-country running, skiing. Have the students create a list of goals they'd like to meet in this activity. (Parental supervision will be needed for some activities.) Students can also include any of the following in their project: safety tips for the sports or activity, instructions on how to perform a task or skill related to the activity, a map, a photo essay, or a journal. Have students present their reports to the class.

Name _____

Running/Walking Improvement Log

Set fitness goals for yourself in the space provided. Then fill in the distance and time of your running or walking activity.

	Distance Goal	Time Goal	Actual Distance	Actual Time
Week 1				
Week 2				
Week 3				
Week 4				
Week 5				
Week 6				
Week 7				
Week 8				
Week 9				
Week 10				
Week 11				
Week 12				

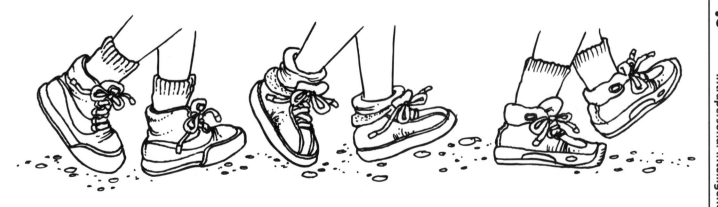

reproducible

FS23284 · Multiple Intelligences Grade 5

Target Your Heart

Choose an activity listed in the chart below. Perform the activity for 2 to 5 minutes. Then feel your pulse to determine the number of heartbeats per minute. Check the heart-rate chart to see if you are in your target range. Try the other activities to see how they affect your heart.

Age	Beats Per Minute
9	148–211
10	147–210
11	146–209
12	145–208

Activity	Beats Per Minute	Target? (yes or no)
jumping jacks		
sit-ups		
jogging in place		
push-ups		
basketball		
weightlifting		
jumping rope		
soccer		
field hockey		
football		
other		

ANSWERS

Page 44: Mystery Equations

a. $(24 \div 3) - 1 = 7$ or $8 - 1 = 7$

b. $65 - (2 \times 6) = 53$ or
$65 - 12 = 53$

c. $400 \div (8 \times 5) = 10$ or
$400 \div 40 = 10$

d. $(103 + 23) - 100 = 26$ or
$126 - 100 = 26$

e. $6 \times (2 + 4) = 36$ or
$6 \times 6 = 36$

f. $(22 + 101) \times 0 = 0$ or
$123 \times 0 = 0$

g. $(42 \div 7) + (21 \div 3) = 13$ or
$6 + 7 = 13$

h. $(6 \times 0) + (12 \times 3) = 36$ or
$0 + 36 = 36$

i. $(4 + 4) + (6 \times 6) = 44$ or
$8 + 36 = 44$

j. $(6 \div 3) + (6 - 3) + (6 + 3) = 14$; or $2 + 3 + 9 = 14$

k. $(100 \div 10) \times (50 \div 10) = 50$ or $10 \times 5 = 50$

l. $(3 \times 4) + (5 + 6) + (8 - 7) = 24$ or $12 + 11 + 1 = 24$

Page 46: Catch the Cat

1. Lily   2. Max

3. Chloe   4. Tiger

5. Sylvia   6. Leo

Page 47: Toothpick Transformations

1.

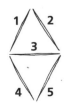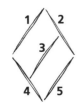

2.

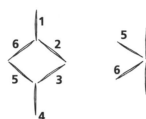

3.

Page 56: Science Analogies

1. caterpillar; A frog develops from a tadpole. A butterfly develops from a caterpillar.

2. toad; Rattlesnake and alligator belong to the same animal family. A toad and a salamander are in the same family.

3. quartz; Sandstone is a kind of sedimentary rock; quartz is a kind of metamorphic rock.

4. dinosaur; Astronomy is the study of stars and paleontology is the study of dinosaurs.

5. heart; The lungs control respiration, and the heart controls circulation.

6. monkey; A snake is a cold-blooded animal. A monkey is a warm-blooded animal.

7. Pluto; Mercury and Venus are inner planets. Uranus and Pluto are outer planets.

8. ice; An avalanche is moving snow. A glacier is moving ice.

9. penicillin; Curie discovered radium. Fleming discovered penicillin.

10. liter; Centimeter and inch are metric and standard measurements of length. Liter and quart are metric and standard measurements for volume.

Page 66: All That Jazz

1. Charlie Parker

2. Louis Armstrong

3. Earl "Fatha" Hines

4. Dizzy Gillespie

5. Fats Waller

6. Lester Young

7. Count Basie

8. Ella Fitzgerald